Contents

Monkey

EASY

Finished Size: 7" (18 cm) tall (seated)

SHOPPING LIST

Yarn

(Medium Weight) 

[7 ounces, 364 yards

(198 grams, 333 meters) per skein]:

- ☐ Brown - 50 yards (45.5 meters)
- ☐ Tan - 65 yards (59.5 meters)

(Light Weight) 

[1.75 ounces, 161 yards

(50 grams, 147 meters) per skein]:

- ☐ Yellow - 10 yards (9.1 meters)
- ☐ Off White - 4 yards (3.7 meters)
- ☐ Black - small amount

Crochet Hooks

- ☐ Size G (4 mm)
  or size needed for gauge
- ☐ Size D (3.25 mm) (banana only)

Additional Supplies

- ☐ 10mm Safety eyes - 2
- ☐ Polyester fiberfill
- ☐ Chenille stems - 2
- ☐ Yarn needle

GAUGE INFORMATION

8 sc and 8 rows/rnds = 2" (5 cm)

Gauge Swatch: 2" (5 cm) square

Ch 9.

Row 1: Sc in second ch from hook and in each ch across: 8 sc.

Rows 2-8: Ch 1, turn; sc in each sc across.

Finish off.

STITCH GUIDE

SINGLE CROCHET 2 TOGETHER ***(abbreviated sc2tog)***

Pull up a loop in each of next 2 sts, YO and draw through all 3 loops on hook **(counts as one sc)** ***(Fig. A)***.

Fig. A

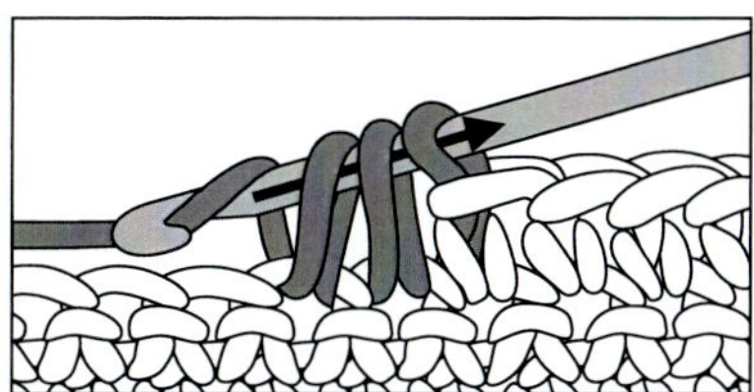

SMALL BOBBLE (uses one sc)

★ YO, insert hook in sc indicated, YO and pull up a loop, YO and draw through 2 loops on hook; repeat from ★ 3 times **more**, YO and draw through all 5 loops on hook **(counts as one st)**.

BOBBLE (uses one sc)

★ YO, insert hook in sc indicated, YO and pull up a loop, YO and draw through 2 loops on hook; repeat from ★ 4 times **more**, YO and draw through all 6 loops on hook **(counts as one st)**.

HEAD

Rnd 1 (Right side)**:** With Brown, make an adjustable ring ***(Figs. 2a-d, pages 48)***, 6 sc in ring; do **not** join, place marker to indicated the beginning of the round ***(see Markers, page 48)***.

Note: Loop a short piece of yarn around any stitch to mark Rnd 1 as **right** side.

Rnd 2: 2 Sc in each sc around: 12 sc.

Rnd 3: (2 Sc in next sc, sc in next sc) around: 18 sc.

Rnds 4 and 5: (Sc in next 2 sc, 2 sc in next sc) around: 32 sc.

Rnd 6: Sc in each sc around.

Rnd 7: (2 Sc in next sc, sc in next 3 sc) around: 40 sc.

Rnds 8 and 9: Sc in each sc around.

Rnd 10: (2 Sc in next sc, sc in next 7 sc) around: 45 sc.

Rnds 11-13: Sc in each sc around.

Rnd 14: (Sc2tog, sc in next 3 sc) around: 36 sc.

Rnd 15: Sc in each sc around.

Rnd 16: (Sc2tog, sc in next 2 sc) around: 27 sc.

Rnd 17: Sc in each sc around.

Stuff Head with polyester fiberfill.

Rnds 18 and 19: (Sc2tog, sc in next sc) around: 12 sc.

Do **not** finish off.

BODY

Rnd 1 (Right side)**:** Sc in each sc around.

Rnd 2: (Sc in next sc, 2 sc in next sc) around: 18 sc.

Rnd 3: (2 Sc in next sc, sc in next 2 sc) around: 24 sc.

Rnd 4: Sc in each sc around.

Rnd 5: (2 Sc in next sc, sc in next 3 sc) around: 30 sc.

Rnds 6 and 7: Sc in each sc around.

Rnd 8: (2 Sc in next sc, sc in next 4 sc) around: 36 sc.

Rnds 9 and 10: Sc in each sc around.

Rnd 11: (Sc2tog, sc in next 4 sc) around: 30 sc.

Rnd 12: Sc in each sc around.

Rnd 13: (Sc2tog, sc in next 3 sc) around: 24 sc.

Rnd 14: Sc in each sc around.

Rnd 15: (Sc2tog, sc in next 2 sc) around: 18 sc.

Rnd 16: (Sc2tog, sc in next sc) around: 12 sc.

Stuff Body with polyester fiberfill.

Rnd 17: Sc2tog around; slip st in next sc, finish off leaving an 8" (20.5 cm) end for sewing.

Thread yarn needle with end and weave yarn through Front Loop Only of remaining sc to close ***(Fig. 4, page 48)***; secure end.

MUZZLE

Rnd 1 (Right side)**:** With Tan, ch 4; 2 sc in second ch from hook, sc in next ch, 3 sc in last ch; working in free loops of beginning ch ***(Fig. 5b, page 49)***, sc in next 2 chs; do **not** join, place marker to indicate the beginning of the round: 8 sc.

Note: Mark Rnd 1 as **right** side.

Rnd 2: 2 Sc in each of next 2 sc, hdc in next sc, 2 sc in each of next 3 sc, hdc in next sc, 2 sc in next sc: 14 sts.

Rnd 3: ★ (2 Sc in next st, sc in next st) twice, hdc in next 2 sts, sc in next st; repeat from ★ once **more**: 18 sts.

Rnd 4: ★ 2 Sc in next st, sc in next 4 sts, 2 sc in next st, sc in next 3 sts; repeat from ★ once **more**: 22 sc.

Rnd 5: Sc in next 4 sc, sc2tog, sc in next 9 sc, sc2tog, sc in next 5 sc; remove marker, sc in next 5 sc, do **not** finish off: 20 sc.

MASK

Row 1 (Right side)**:** Working in Front Loops Only, (slip st, ch 2, 2 dc) in next sc, hdc in next 2 sc, sc in next 2 sc, hdc in next 2 sc, 2 dc in next dc, leaving remaining sts unworked: 10 sts.

Row 2: Ch 2 (does **not** count as a st), turn; working in both loops, dc in first dc, 2 dc in next dc, hdc in next 6 sts, 2 dc in next dc, (dc, ch 2, slip st) in last dc: 12 sts.

Row 3: Ch 3 (does **not** count as a st), turn; skip ch-2 and sc in first 3 dc, hdc in next 6 hdc, sc in next 3 dc, ch 2, slip st in base of turning ch on Row 2; finish off leaving a 16" (40.5 cm) length for sewing.

Attach safety eyes between hdc on Row 1 of Mask.

Using satin stitch and Brown ***(Fig. 8a, page 50)***, add nostrils angled across Rnd 3 of Muzzle; add Eyebrows using straight stitch ***(Fig. 9, page 50).***

EAR (Make 2)

INNER

Row 1: With Tan, make an adjustable ring, 7 sc in ring; do **not** join.

Row 2 (Right side)**:** Ch 1, turn; hdc in first sc, (2 hdc in next sc, hdc in next sc) 3 times; finish off: 10 hdc.

Note: Mark Row 2 as **right** side.

OUTER

Row 1: With Brown, make an adjustable ring, 7 sc in ring; do **not** join.

Row 2 (Right side)**:** Ch 1, turn; hdc in first sc, (2 hdc in next sc, hdc in next sc) 3 times; do **not** finish off: 10 hdc.

Joining Rnd: Ch 1, turn; holding **wrong** sides together, Inner Ear facing you, and working through **both** loops on **both** pieces, 2 sc in first hdc, sc in next 8 hdc, 2 sc in last hdc; ch 1, working through **both** pieces, work 4 sc across end of rows, ch 1; join with slip st to first sc, finish off leaving a 10" (25.5 cm) length for sewing.

FOOT & LEFT LEG

Rnd 1 (Right side)**:** With Tan, ch 4; 2 sc in second ch from hook, sc in next ch, 3 sc in last ch; working in free loops of beginning ch, sc in next 2 chs; do **not** join, place marker to indicate the beginning of the round: 8 sc.

Note: Mark Rnd 1 as **right** side.

Rnd 2: (2 Sc in next sc, sc in next 3 sc) twice: 10 sc.

Rnd 3: 2 Sc in next sc, sc in next 9 sc: 11 sc.

Rnds 4 and 5: Sc in each sc around.

Rnd 6: Sc in next 2 sc, work Bobble in next sc (thumb), sc in next 8 sc.

Rnd 7: Sc in next 2 sc, sc2tog, sc in next 7 sc; remove marker, sc in next 2 sc, slip st in next sc changing to Brown *(Fig. 6a, page 49)*: 10 sts.

Rnd 8: Ch 1, sc in same st as slip st and in each st around; do **not** join, place marker to indicate the beginning of the round.

Rnds 9-11: Sc in each sc around.

Rnd 12: Sc in next 4 sc, 2 sc in next sc, sc in next 5 sc: 11 sc.

Rnds 13 and 14: Sc in each sc around.

Rnd 15: Sc in next 2 sc, 2 sc in next sc, sc in next 5 sc, hdc in next 3 sc (knee): 12 sts.

Rnd 16: Hdc in next 2 sc, sc in next 10 sts.

Rnd 17 and 18: Sc in each st around.

Rnd 19: Sc in next 10 sc; remove marker.

Do **not** add polyester fiberfill to Foot & Leg so piece is more agile.

Joining Row: Ch 1; flatten top of Leg having ch at fold. Working through **both** loops of **both** sides (***Fig. 4, page 48)***, sc2tog, sc in next 2 sts, sc2tog; finish off leaving an 8" (20.5 cm) length for sewing.

FOOT & RIGHT LEG

Work same as Foot & Left Leg through Rnd 14: 11 sc.

Rnd 15: 2 Sc in next sc, sc in next 2 sc, hdc in next 5 sc (knee), sc in next 3 sc: 12 sts.

Rnds 16-18: Sc in each sc around.

Rnd 19: Sc in next 10 sc; remove marker.

Do **not** add polyester fiberfill to Foot & Leg so piece is more agile.

Joining Row: Ch 1; flatten top of Leg having ch at fold. Working through **both** loops of **both** sides, sc2tog, sc in next 2 sts, sc2tog; finish off leaving an 8" (20.5 cm) length for sewing.

HAND & ARM (Make 2)

Rnd 1 (Right side)**:** With Tan, ch 3; 2 sc in second ch from hook, 3 sc in last ch; working in free loops of beginning ch, sc in next ch; do **not** join, place marker to indicate the beginning of the round: 6 sc.

Note: Mark Rnd 1 as **right** side.

Rnd 2: (2 Sc in next sc, sc in next 2 sc) twice: 8 sc.

Rnd 3: 2 Sc in next sc, sc in next 7 sc: 9 sc.

Rnd 4: Sc in each sc around.

Rnd 5: Sc in next sc, work Small Bobble in next sc (thumb), sc in next 7 sc.

Rnd 6: Sc in next sc, sc2tog, sc in next 6 sc; remove marker, sc in next sc, slip st in next sc changing to Brown: 8 sts.

Rnd 7: Ch 1, sc in same st as slip st and in each st around; do **not** join, place marker to indicate the beginning of the round.

Rnds 8-10: Sc in each sc around.

Rnd 11: Sc in next 3 sc, 2 sc in next sc, sc in next 4 sc: 9 sc.

Rnds 12-14: Sc in each sc around.

Rnd 15: 2 Sc in next sc, sc in next 5 sc, hdc in next 3 sc (elbow): 10 sts.

Rnd 16: Hdc in next sc, sc in next 9 sts.

Rnds 17 and 18: Sc in each st around.

Do **not** add polyester fiberfill to Hand & Arm so piece is more agile.

Joining Row: Ch 1; flatten top of Arm having ch at fold. Working through **both** loops of **both** sides, sc in first st, sc2tog, sc in last 2 sts; finish off leaving an 8" (20.5 cm) length for sewing.

CHEST

Rnd 1 (Right side)**:** With Tan, ch 7; 2 dc in fourth ch from hook **(3 skipped chs count as first dc)**, dc in next 2 chs, 6 dc in last ch; working in free loops of beginning ch, dc in next 2 chs, 3 dc in next ch; join with slip st to first dc: 16 dc.

Note: Mark Rnd 1 as **right** side.

Rnd 2: Ch 2, hdc in next 2 dc, 2 hdc in next dc, hdc in next dc, 2 hdc in each of next 2 dc, 3 hdc in each of next 2 dc, 2 hdc in each of next 2 dc, hdc in next dc, 2 hdc in next dc, hdc in next 2 dc, ch 2, slip st in next dc and in next slip st; finish off leaving a 12" (30.5 cm) length for sewing.

TAIL

Rnd 1 (Right side)**:** With Brown, make an adjustable ring, 4 sc in ring; do **not** join, place marker to indicated the beginning of the round.

Note: Mark Rnd 1 as **right** side.

Rnd 2: (2 Sc in next sc, sc in next sc) twice: 6 sc.

Insert 2 folded and twisted chenille stems into piece. Sc in sts around outside of stems.

Rnds 3-20: Sc in each sc around.

Rnd 21: 2 Sc in next sc, sc in each sc around: 7 sc.

Rnds 22 and 23: Sc in each sc around.

Rnd 24: Sc in next 3 sc, 2 sc in next sc, sc in next 3 sc: 8 sc.

Rnd 25: (Sc in next sc, 2 sc in next sc) around: 12 sc.

Rnd 26: Sc in each sc around; slip st in next sc, finish off leaving a 10" (25.5 cm) length for sewing.

BANANA

Note: Use smaller size hook for banana.

Rnd 1 (Right side)**:** With Black, make an adjustable ring, 5 sc in ring; join with slip st to first sc changing to Yellow, cut Black.

Note: Mark Rnd 1 as **right** side.

Rnd 2: Ch 1, sc in same st as joining and in next 3 sc, 2 sc in last sc; join with slip st to first sc: 6 sc.

Rnd 3: Ch 1, sc in same st as joining, 2 sc in next sc, (sc in next sc, 2 sc in next sc) twice; do **not** join, place marker to indicate the beginning of the round: 9 sc.

Rnds 4-6: 2 Sc in next sc, sc in each sc around: 12 sc.

Rnds 7-12: Sc in each sc around.

First Peel-Row 1: Sc in Front Loop Only of next 4 sc, leave remaining 8 sc unworked.

Rows 2-4: Ch 1, turn; sc in both loops of first 4 sc.

Row 5: Ch 1, turn; sc in first sc, sc2tog, sc in last sc: 3 sc.

Row 6: Ch 1, turn; sc in first sc, skip next sc, sc in last sc: 2 sc.

Row 7: Ch 1, turn; beginning in first sc, sc2tog; finish off: one sc.

Second Peel-Row 1: With **right** side facing and working in Front Loops Only, join Yellow with sc in next sc on Rnd 12 ***(Fig. 5a, page 49)***; sc in next 3 sc, leave remaining 4 sc unworked.

Complete same as first Peel.

Third Peel-Row 1: With **right** side facing and working in Front Loops Only, join Yellow with sc in next sc on Rnd 12; sc in next 3 sc.

Complete same as first Peel.

FLESH

Rnd 1: With **right** side facing and working in free loops on Rnd 12, join Off White with sc in first loop; sc in each loop around; do **not** join, place marker to indicate the beginning of the round: 12 sc.

Rnd 2: Sc in both loops of each sc around.

Stuff piece lightly with polyester fiberfill as you work.

Rnds 3-5: Sc2tog, sc in each sc around: 9 sc.

Rnd 5: (Sc in next sc, sc2tog) around: 6 sc.

Rnd 6: Sc2tog 3 times; finish off leaving an 8" (20.5 cm) length for sewing.

FINISHING

Using Photo as a guide for placement and using long ends:

- Sew one Arm to each side of Body across Rnds 1-4.
- Sew Legs to bottom of Body across Rnds 15-17, so Monkey is in a seated position.
- Stuff Muzzle with polyester fiberfill. With top of Mask between Rnds 6 & 7 and bottom of Muzzle between Rnds 17 & 18, sew to center of Head.
- Sew Ears on each side of Head across Rnds 8-14 .
- Sew Chest to center of Body from Rnds 3-13.
- Sew Tail to center back of Body across Rnd 10-13.
- With Brown and using straight stitch, add lines to define fingers and toes.
- Sew Banana to right hand; tack Banana to chest if desired.

Panda

EASY

Finished Size: 6½" (16.5 cm) tall (seated)

SHOPPING LIST

Yarn (Medium Weight) 

[7 ounces, 364 yards
(198 grams, 333 meters) per skein]:

- ❑ Soft White - 50 yards (45.5 meters)
- ❑ Black - 65 yards (59.5 meters)
- ❑ Green - 5 yards (4.5 meters)

Crochet Hook

❑ Size G (4 mm)
or size needed for gauge

Additional Supplies

- ❑ 10mm Safety eyes -2
- ❑ Polyester fiberfill
- ❑ Yarn needle

GAUGE INFORMATION

8 sc and 8 rows = 2" (5 cm)

Gauge Swatch: 2" (5 cm) square

Ch 9.

Row 1: Sc in second ch from hook and in each ch across: 8 sc.

Rows 2-8: Ch 1, turn; sc in each sc across.

Finish off.

STITCH GUIDE

SINGLE CROCHET 2 TOGETHER
(abbreviated sc2tog)

Pull up a loop in each of next 2 sts, YO and draw through all 3 loops on hook **(counts as one sc)** ***(Fig. A)***.

Fig. A

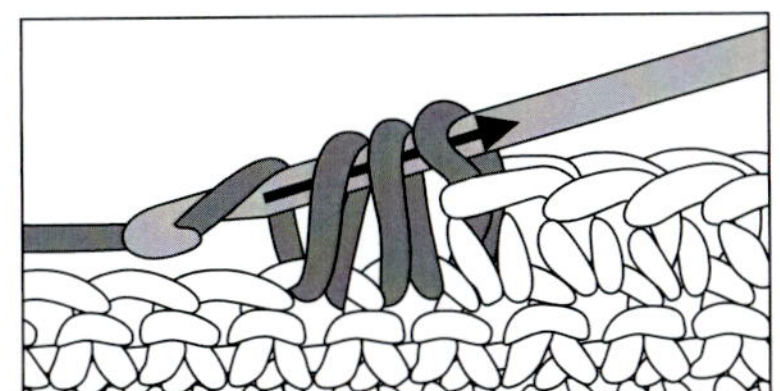

HEAD

Rnd 1 (Right side)**:** With Soft White, make an adjustable ring ***(Figs. 2a-d, pages 48)***, 6 sc in ring; do **not** join, place marker to indicated the beginning of the round ***(see Markers, page 48)***.

Note: Loop a short piece of yarn around any stitch to mark Rnd 1 as **right** side.

Rnd 2: 2 Sc in each sc around: 12 sc.

Rnd 3: (2 Sc in next sc, sc in next sc) around: 18 sc.

Rnds 4 and 5: (Sc in next 2 sc, 2 sc in next sc) around: 32 sc.

Rnd 6: Sc in each sc around.

Rnd 7: (2 Sc in next sc, sc in next 3 sc) around: 40 sc.

Rnds 8-11: Sc in each sc around.

Rnd 11: (Sc2tog, sc in next 3 sc) around: 32 sc.

Rnd 12: (Sc2tog, sc in next 6 sc) around: 28 sc.

Rnd 13: (Sc2tog, sc in next 5 sc) around: 24 sc.

Rnd 14: (Sc2tog, sc in next sc) around: 16 sc.

Rnd 15: Sc in each sc around; slip st in next sc changing to Black ***(Fig. 6a, page 49)***.

Stuff Head with polyester fiberfill.

BODY

Rnd 1 (Right side): Ch 1, sc in same st as slip st, 2 sc in next sc, (sc in next sc, 2 sc in next sc) around; do not join, place marker to indicate the beginning of the round: 24 sc.

Rnd 2: (2 Sc in next sc, 2 sc in next sc) around: 32 sc.

Rnd 3: Sc in each sc around.

Rnd 4: (2 Sc in next sc, sc in next 7 sc) around: 36 sc.

Rnd 5: Sc in each sc around; slip st in next sc changing to Soft White, cut Black.

Rnd 6: Ch 1, sc in same st as slip st and in each sc around; do not join, place marker to indicated the beginning of the rnd.

Rnds 7-11: Sc in each sc around.

Rnd 12: (Sc2tog, sc in next 4 sc) around: 30 sc.

Rnd 13: Sc in each sc around.

Rnd 14: (Sc2tog, sc in next 3 sc) around: 24 sc.

Rnd 15: (Sc2tog, sc in next 2 sc) around: 18 sc.

Rnd 16: (Sc2tog, sc in next sc) around: 12 sc.

Stuff Body with polyester fiberfill.

Rnd 17: Sc2tog around; slip st in next sc, finish off leaving an 8" (20.5 cm) length for sewing.

Thread yarn needle with end and weave yarn through Front Loop Only of remaining sc to close ***(Fig. 4, page 48)***; secure end.

FOOT & LEG (Make 2)

Rnd 1 (Right side)**:** With Black, make an adjustable ring, 6 sc in ring; do **not** join, place marker to indicated the beginning of the round.

Note: Mark Rnd 1 as **right** side.

Rnd 2: 2 Sc in each sc around: 12 sc.

Rnd 3: (2 Sc in next sc, sc in next sc) around: 18 sc.

Rnd 4: (2 Sc in next sc, sc in next 2 sc) around: 24 sc.

Rnd 5: Sc in each sc around.

Rnd 6: Sc in next 12 sc, (sc2tog, sc in next 2 sc) 3 times: 21 sc.

Rnd 7: Sc in next 13 sc, sc2tog 4 times: 17 sc.

Rnd 8: Sc in each sc around.

Rnd 9: Sc in next 11 sc, sc2tog 3 times: 14 sc.

Rnd 10: Sc2tog, (sc in next 2 sc, sc2tog) 3 times: 10 sc.

Stuff Foot with polyester fiberfill.

Rnds 11 and 12: Sc in each sc around.

Rnd 13: Sc in next 8 sc; ch 1, flatten top of Leg having ch at fold. Working through **both** loops of **both** pieces ***(Fig. 4, page 48)***, sc in each st across; finish off leaving an 8" (20.5 cm) length for sewing.

ARM (Make 2)

Rnd 1 (Right side)**:** With Black, make an adjustable ring, 6 sc in ring; do **not** join, place marker to indicated the beginning of the round.

Note: Mark Rnd 1 as **right** side.

Rnd 2: 2 Sc in each sc around: 12 sc.

Rnd 3: (2 Sc in next sc, sc in 2 next sc) around: 16 sc.

Rnds 4 and 5: Sc in each sc around.

Rnd 6: (Sc2tog, sc in next 2 sc) around: 12 sc.

Rnds 7 and 8: Sc in each sc around.

Rnd 9: (Sc2tog, sc in next sc) around: 8 sc.

Stuff Arm with polyester fiberfill.

Rnds 10 and 11: Sc in each sc around.

Joining Row: Ch 1; flatten top of Arm having ch at fold. Working through **both** loops of **both** sides, sc in each st across; finish off leaving an 8" (20.5 cm) length for sewing.

EAR (Make 2)

Rnd 1 (Right side)**:** With Black, ch 4; sc in second ch from hook and in next ch, 3 sc in last ch; working in free loops of beginning ch ***(Fig. 5b, page 49)***, sc in next ch, 2 sc in next ch; do **not** join, place marker to indicate the beginning of the round: 8 sc.

Note: Mark Rnd 1 as **right** side.

Rnd 2: (Sc in next 3 sc, 2 sc in next sc) twice: 10 sc.

Rnd 3: Sc in each sc around.

Joining Row: Ch 1; flatten the Ear having the ch at fold. Working through **both** loops of **both** sides, sc2tog beginning in first sc, sc in next sc, sc2tog; finish off leaving an 8" (20.5 cm) length for sewing.

MUZZLE

Rnd 1 (Right side)**:** With Soft White, make an adjustable ring, work 5 sc in ring; do **not** join, place marker to indicate the beginning of the round.

Note: Mark Rnd 1 as **right** side.

Rnd 2: 2 Sc in each sc around: 10 sc.

Rnd 3: 2 Sc in next sc, sc in next sc, hdc in next sc, (2 hdc in next sc, hdc in next sc) twice, sc in next sc, 2 sc in next sc, sc in next sc: 14 sts.

Rnd 4: Sc in each st around; slip st in next 7 sc, finish off leaving a 10" (25.5 cm) length for sewing.

Using satin stitch ***(Fig. 8b, page 50)***, add Black Nose; using straight stitch ***(Fig. 9, page 50)***, and Black features to Muzzle.

EYE PATCH (Make 2)

With Black, ch 4, 2 sc in second ch from hook, slip st in next ch, 4 sc in last ch; working in free loops of beginning ch, sc in next ch, 2 sc in next ch; join with slip st to first sc, finish off leaving an 8" (20.5 cm) length for sewing.

BAMBOO

First Leaf: With Green, ch 6; working in back ridge of chs *(Fig. 3, page 48)*, slip st in second ch from hook, sc in next ch, hdc in next ch, sc in next ch, slip st in next ch; do **not** finish off.

Second Leaf: Ch 7; working in back ridge of chs, slip st in second ch from hook, sc in next ch, hdc in next 2 chs, sc in next ch, slip st in next ch; do **not** finish off.

Third Leaf: Ch 6; working in back ridge of chs, slip st in second ch from hook, sc in next ch, hdc in next ch, sc in next ch, slip st in next ch; skip second Leaf and slip st in ch at base of First Leaf; do **not** finish off.

Stalk: Ch 12; sc in second ch from hook and in next 10 chs, ch 1; rotate Leaves keeping ch behind them, slip st in free loops of next 11 chs; finish off leaving a 10" (25.5 cm) length for sewing.

Thread yarn needle with long end. To sew Stalk together, insert needle in **both** loops of first slip st **and** the corresponding sc on the opposite side, tighten yarn causing stalk to fold, ★ insert needle in **both** loops of next slip st **and** the corresponding sc on the opposite side, tighten yarn; repeat from ★ across to base of Leaves; secure end.

FINISHING

Using Photo as a guide for placement and using long ends:

- Sew one Arm to each side of Body across Rnds 1-3.
- Sew Legs to bottom of Body across Rnds 13-16, so Panda is in a seated position.
- Stuff Muzzle with polyester fiberfill and sew to center of Head, across Rnds 8-13.
- Attach safety eyes to Eye Patches; sew at an angle on each side of Muzzle, beginning at Rnd 6 or 7.
- Sew Ears to each side of Head, across Rnds 4-8.
- Sew Bamboo to Hand.

Brown Bear

EASY

Finished Size: 5½" (14 cm) tall (seated)

SHOPPING LIST

Yarn (Medium Weight) 

[5 ounces, 256 yards (141 grams, 234 meters) per skein**]:**

- ☐ Brown - 100 yards (91.5 meters)

[7 ounces, 364 yards (198 grams, 333 meters) per skein**]:**

- ☐ White - 5 yards (4.5 meters)
- ☐ Black - 2 yards (1.8 meters)

Crochet Hook

- ☐ Size G (4 mm) **or** size needed for gauge

Additional Supplies

- ☐ Polyester fiberfill
- ☐ Yarn needle

GAUGE INFORMATION

8 sc and 8 rows = 2" (5 cm)

Gauge Swatch: 2" (5 cm) square

Ch 9.

Row 1: Sc in second ch from hook and in each ch across: 8 sc.

Rows 2-8: Ch 1, turn; sc in each sc across.

Finish off.

STITCH GUIDE

SINGLE CROCHET 2 TOGETHER

(abbreviated sc2tog)

Pull up a loop in each of next 2 sts, YO and draw through all 3 loops on hook **(counts as one sc)** ***(Fig. A)***.

Fig. A

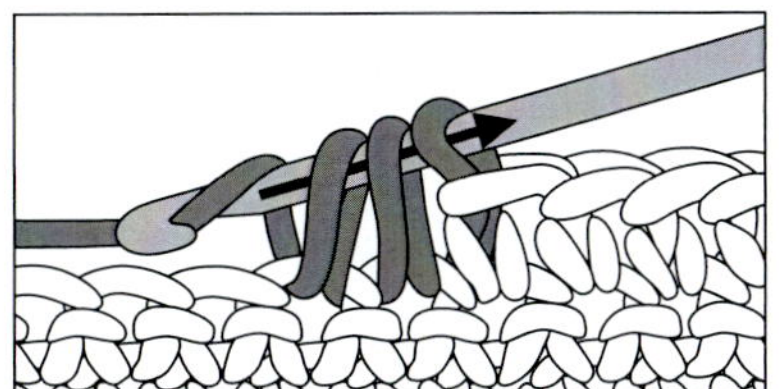

HEAD & BODY

Rnd 1 (Right side)**:** With Brown, make an adjustable ring ***(Figs. 2a-d, pages 48)***, 6 sc in ring; do **not** join, place marker to indicated the beginning of the round ***(see Markers, page 48)***.

Note: Loop a short piece of yarn around any stitch to mark Rnd 1 as **right** side.

Rnd 2: 2 Sc in each sc around: 12 sc.

Rnd 3: (2 Sc in next sc, sc in next sc) around: 18 sc.

Rnd 4: (2 Sc in next sc, sc in next 2 sc) around: 24 sc.

Rnd 5: (2 Sc in next sc, sc in next 3 sc) around: 30 sc.

Rnds 6-9: Sc in each sc around.

Rnd 10: (Sc2tog, sc in next 3 sc) around: 24 sc.

Rnd 11: (Sc2tog, sc in next 2 sc) around: 18 sc.

Rnd 12: (Sc2tog, sc in next sc) around: 12 sc.

Stuff Head with polyester fiberfill.

Rnd 13: (2 Sc in next sc, sc in next sc) around: 18 sc.

Rnd 14: (2 Sc in next sc, sc in next 2 sc) around: 24 sc.

Rnd 15: (2 Sc in next sc, sc in next 3 sc) around: 30 sc.

Rnd 16: (2 Sc in next sc, sc in next 4 sc) around: 36 sc.

Rnds 17-24: Sc in each sc around.

Rnd 25: (Sc2tog, sc in next 4 sc) around: 30 sc.

Rnd 26: (Sc2tog, sc in next 3 sc) around: 24 sc.

Rnd 27: (Sc2tog, sc in next 2 sc) around: 18 sc.

Rnd 28: (Sc2tog, sc in next sc) around: 12 sc.

Stuff Body with polyester fiberfill.

Rnd 29: Sc2tog around; slip st in next sc, finish off leaving a 6" (15 cm) length for sewing.

Thread yarn needle with end and weave yarn through Front Loop Only of remaining sc to close ***(Fig. 4, page 48)***; secure end.

FOOT & LEG (Make 2)

Rnd 1 (Right side)**:** With Brown, make an adjustable ring, 6 sc in ring; do **not** join, place marker to indicated the beginning of the round.

Note: Mark Rnd 1 as **right** side.

Rnd 2: 2 Sc in each sc around: 12 sc.

Rnd 3: (2 Sc in next sc, sc in next sc) around: 18 sc.

Rnd 4: (2 Sc in next sc, sc in next 2 sc) around: 24 sc.

Rnd 5: Sc in each sc around.

Rnd 6: Sc in next 12 sc, (sc2tog, sc in next 2 sc) 3 times: 21 sc.

Rnd 7: Sc in next 13 sc, sc2tog 4 times: 17 sc.

Rnd 8: Sc in each sc around.

Rnd 9: Sc in next 11 sc, sc2tog 3 times: 14 sc.

Rnd 10: Sc2tog, (sc in next 2 sc, sc2tog) 3 times: 10 sc.

Stuff Foot with polyester fiberfill.

Rnds 11 and 12: Sc in each sc around.

Rnd 13: Sc in next 8 sc; ch 1, flatten top of Leg having ch at fold. Working through **both** loops of **both** pieces *(Fig. 4, page 48)*, sc in each st across; finish off leaving an 8" (20.5 cm) length for sewing.

ARM (Make 2)

Rnd 1 (Right side)**:** With Brown, make an adjustable ring, 6 sc in ring; do **not** join, place marker to indicated the beginning of the round.

Note: Mark Rnd 1 as **right** side.

Rnd 2: 2 Sc in each sc around: 12 sc.

Rnd 3: (2 Sc in next sc, sc in next sc) around: 18 sc.

Rnds 4 and 5: Sc in each sc around.

Rnd 6 (Decrease rnd)**:** (Sc2tog, sc in next sc) around: 12 sc.

Rnds 7-9: Repeat Rnds 4-6: 8 sc.

Stuff Arm with polyester fiberfill.

Rnds 10 and 11: Sc in each sc around.

Joining Row: Ch 1; flatten top of Arm having ch at fold. Working through **both** loops of **both** pieces, sc in each st across; finish off leaving an 8" (20.5 cm) length for sewing.

EAR (Make 2)

With Brown, ch 5.

Row 1: Sc in back ridge of second ch from hook and each ch across *(Fig. 3, page 48)*: 4 sc.

Row 2 (Right side)**:** Ch 1, turn; sc in first sc, (hdc, 2 dc, tr) in next sc *(Figs. 15a & b, page 51)*, (tr, 2 dc, hdc) in next sc, sc in last sc; ch 1, working in free loops of beginning ch *(Fig. 5b, page 49)*, sc in each ch across, ch 1; join with slip st to first sc, finish off leaving a 6" (15 cm) length for sewing.

Note: Mark Row 2 as **right** side.

MUZZLE

Rnd 1 (Right side)**:** With White, ch 2, (3 sc, 3 hdc) in second ch from hook; do **not** join, place marker to indicated the beginning of the round: 6 sts.

Note: Mark Rnd 1 as **right** side.

Rnd 2: 2 Sc in each of next 3 sc, (sc, hdc) in next hdc, 2 hdc in next hdc, (hdc, sc) in next hdc: 12 sts.

Rnd 3: (2 Sc in next st, sc in next st) around: 18 sc.

Rnd 4: Sc in each sc around.

Rnd 5: Slip st in each sc around; slip st in next sc, finish off leaving a 12" (30.5 cm) length for sewing.

TAIL

With Brown, ch 4; working in back ridge of chs, sc in second ch from hook, hdc in last 2 chs; finish off leaving a 6" (15 cm) length for sewing.

FINISHING

Using Photo as a guide for placement:

- Sew one Arm to each side of Body across Rnds 15-22.
- Sew one Ear to each side of Head.
- Sew Legs to bottom of Body so Bear is in a seated position; sew Tail to back of Body.
- Using satin stitch *(Fig. 8b, page 50)*, add White pads to bottom of each foot and to belly.
- Using satin stitch *(Fig. 8a, page 50)* and straight stitch *(Fig. 9, page 50)*, add Black eyes, Nose and features.

Hippo

EASY

Finished Size: 6" (15 cm) tall (seated)

SHOPPING LIST

Yarn (Medium Weight) 

[7 ounces, 364 yards (198 grams, 333 meters) per skein]:

- ☐ Grey - 75 yards (68.5 meters)
- ☐ Black - 2 yards (1.8 meters)
- ☐ Lt Grey - 1 yard (.9 meter)

Crochet Hook

- ☐ Size G (4 mm) **or** size needed for gauge

Additional Supplies

- ☐ Polyester fiberfill
- ☐ Yarn needle

GAUGE INFORMATION

8 sc and 8 rows = 2" (5 cm)

Gauge Swatch: 2" (5 cm) square

Ch 9.

Row 1: Sc in second ch from hook and in each ch across: 8 sc.

Rows 2-8: Ch 1, turn; sc in each sc across.

Finish off.

STITCH GUIDE

SINGLE CROCHET 2 TOGETHER

(abbreviated sc2tog)

Pull up a loop in each of next 2 sts, YO and draw through all 3 loops on hook **(counts as one sc)** ***(Fig. A)***.

Fig. A

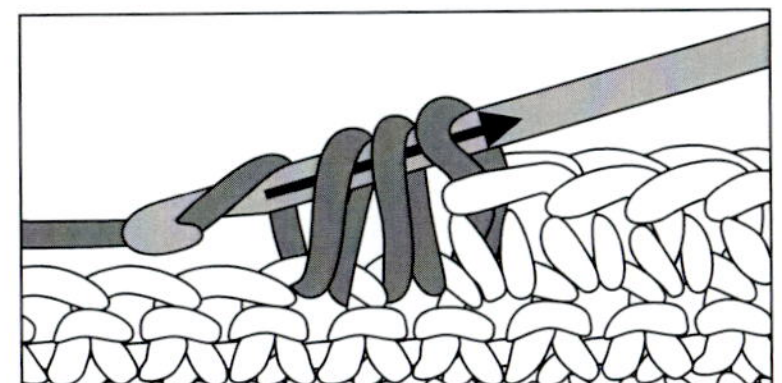

HEAD & BODY

Rnd 1 (Right side)**:** With Grey, make an adjustable ring ***(Figs. 2a-d, pages 48)***, 6 sc in ring; do **not** join, place marker to indicated the beginning of the round ***(see Markers, page 48)***.

Note: Loop a short piece of yarn around any stitch to mark Rnd 1 as **right** side.

Rnd 2: 2 Sc in each sc around: 12 sc.

Rnd 3: (2 Sc in next sc, sc in next sc) around: 18 sc.

Rnd 4: (2 Sc in next sc, sc in next 2 sc) around: 24 sc.

Rnd 5: (2 Sc in next sc, sc in next 3 sc) around: 30 sc.

Rnds 6-10: Sc in each sc around.

Rnd 11: (Sc2tog, sc in next 3 sc) around: 24 sc.

Rnd 12: (Sc2tog, sc in next 2 sc) around: 18 sc.

Rnd 13: (Sc2tog, sc in next sc) around: 12 sc.

Stuff Head with polyester fiberfill.

Rnd 14: (2 Sc in next sc, sc in next sc) around: 18 sc.

Rnd 15: (2 Sc in next sc, sc in next 2 sc) around: 24 sc.

Rnd 16: (2 Sc in next sc, sc in next 3 sc) around: 30 sc.

Rnd 17: (2 Sc in next sc, sc in next 4 sc) around: 36 sc.

Rnds 18-25: Sc in each sc around.

Rnd 26: (Sc2tog, sc in next 4 sc) around: 30 sc.

Rnd 27: (Sc2tog, sc in next 3 sc) around: 24 sc.

Rnd 28: (Sc2tog, sc in next 2 sc) around: 18 sc.

Rnd 29: (Sc2tog, sc in next sc) around: 12 sc.

Stuff Body with polyester fiberfill.

Rnd 30: Sc2tog around; slip st in next sc, finish off leaving a 6" (15 cm) length for sewing.

Thread yarn needle with end and weave yarn through Front Loop Only of remaining sc to close ***(Fig. 4, page 48)***; secure end.

FOOT & LEG (Make 2)

Rnd 1 (Right side)**:** With Grey, make an adjustable ring, 6 sc in ring; do **not** join, place marker to indicated the beginning of the round.

Note: Mark Rnd 1 as **right** side.

Rnd 2: 2 Sc in each sc around: 12 sc.

Rnd 3: (2 Sc in next sc, sc in next sc) around: 18 sc.

Rnd 4: (2 Sc in next sc, sc in next 5 sc) 3 times: 21 sc.

Rnd 5: Sc in each sc around.

Rnd 6: (Sc2tog, sc in next 5 sc) 3 times: 18 sc.

Rnd 7: Sc in each sc around.

Rnd 8: (Sc2tog, sc in next 4 sc) 3 times; slip st in next sc, finish off leaving an 8" (20.5 cm) length for sewing: 15 sts.

Stuff Foot & Leg with polyester fiberfill.

ARM (Make 2)

Rnd 1 (Right side)**:** With Grey, make an adjustable ring, 5 sc in ring; do **not** join, place marker to indicated the beginning of the round.

Note: Mark Rnd 1 as **right** side.

Rnd 2: 2 Sc in each sc around: 10 sc.

Rnd 3: (2 Sc in next sc, sc in next sc) around: 15 sc.

Rnds 4 and 5: Sc in each sc around.

Rnd 6: (Sc2tog, sc in next 3 sc) 3 times: 12 sc.

Rnd 7: Sc in each sc around.

Rnd 8: (Sc2tog, sc in next 4 sc) twice: 10 sc.

Rnds 9-11: Sc in each sc around.

Stuff Arm with polyester fiberfill.

Joining Row: Ch 1; flatten top of Arm having ch at fold. Working through **both** loops of **both** sides ***(Fig. 4, page 48)***, sc in each st across; finish off leaving an 8" (20.5 cm) length for sewing.

EAR (Make 2)

Rnd 1 (Right side)**:** With Grey, make an adjustable ring, 5 sc in ring; do **not** join, place marker to indicated the beginning of the round.

Note: Mark Rnd 1 as **right** side.

Rnd 2: 2 Sc in each sc around: 10 sc.

Rnds 3 and 4: Sc in each sc around; at end of Rnd 4, slip st in next sc, finish off leaving a 6" (15 cm) length for sewing.

SNOUT

Rnd 1 (Right side)**:** With Grey, ch 4; 2 sc in second ch from hook, sc in next ch, 3 sc in last ch; working in free loops of beginning ch ***(Fig. 5b, page 49)***, sc in next 2 chs; do **not** join, place marker to indicate the beginning of the round: 8 sc.

Note: Mark Rnd 1 as **right** side.

Rnd 2: 2 Sc in each of next 2 sc, sc in next sc, 2 sc in each of next 3 sc, sc in next sc, 2 sc in next sc: 14 sc.

Rnd 3: (2 Sc in next sc, sc in next sc, 2 sc in next sc, sc in next 4 sc) twice: 18 sc.

Rnd 4: Sc in next 2 sc, 2 sc in next sc, sc in next 8 sc, 2 sc in next sc, sc in next 6 sc: 20 sc.

Rnd 5: (Sc in next sc, 2 sc in next sc) 3 times, sc in next 5 sc, 2 sc in next sc, (sc in next sc, 2 sc in next sc) twice, sc in next 4 sc: 26 sc.

Rnd 6: Sc in each sc around.

Rnd 7: (Sc in next sc, sc2tog) 3 times, sc in next 5 sc, sc2tog, (sc in next sc, sc2tog) twice, sc in next 4 sc: 20 sc.

Rnd 8: (Sc in next 2 sc, sc2tog) twice, sc in next 4 sc, sc2tog, sc in next sc, sc2tog, sc in next 3 sc: 16 sc.

Rnd 9: Sc in each sc around; slip st in next sc, finish off leaving a 10" (25.5 cm) length for sewing.

FINISHING

Using Photo as a guide for placement and using long ends:

- Sew one Arm to each side of Body across sts on Rnd 15.
- Flatten Ear having long end at fold; sew fold on each side of last rnd together and sew to each side of Head.
- Sew Legs to Body across Rnds 23-27 so Hippo is in a seated position.
- Using satin stitch ***(Fig. 8a, page 50)***, add Lt Grey nostrils to Snout; stuff Snout lightly and sew to center of face, across Rnds 9-13.
- Using satin stitch, add Black eyes across Rnds 7 and 8, having 3 to 4 sts between eyes.

Giraffe

EASY

Finished Size: 8" (20.5 cm) tall (seated)

SHOPPING LIST

Yarn (Medium Weight) 

[7 ounces, 364 yards
(198 grams, 333 meters) per skein]:

☐ Gold - 86 yards (78.5 meters)

☐ Black - 2 yards (1.8 meters)

[5 ounces, 256 yards
(141 grams, 234 meters) per skein]:

☐ Brown - 18 yards (16.5 meters)

Crochet Hook

☐ Size G (4 mm)
or size needed for gauge

Additional Supplies

☐ Polyester fiberfill

☐ Yarn needle

GAUGE INFORMATION

8 sc and 8 rows = 2" (5 cm)

Gauge Swatch: 2" (5 cm) square

Ch 9.

Row 1: Sc in second ch from hook and in each ch across: 8 sc.

Rows 2-8: Ch 1, turn; sc in each sc across.

Finish off.

STITCH GUIDE

SINGLE CROCHET 2 TOGETHER
(abbreviated sc2tog)

Pull up a loop in each of next 2 sts, YO and draw through all 3 loops on hook **(counts as one sc)** ***(Fig. A)***.

Fig. A

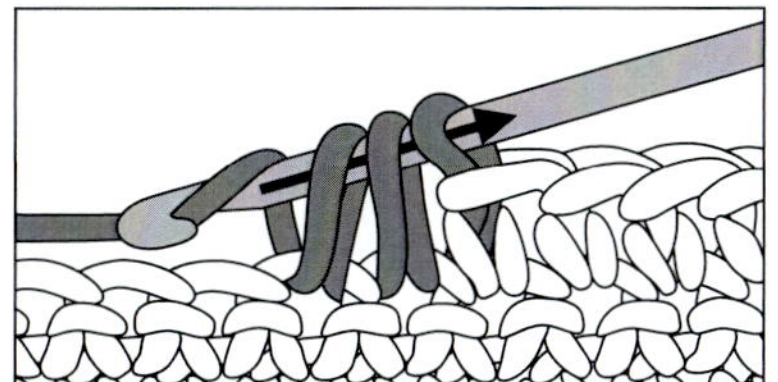

HEAD & BODY

Rnd 1 (Right side)**:** With Gold, make an adjustable ring ***(Figs. 2a-d, pages 48)***, 6 sc in ring; do **not** join, place marker to indicated the beginning of the round ***(see Markers, page 48)***.

Note: Loop a short piece of yarn around any stitch to mark Rnd 1 as **right** side.

Rnd 2: 2 Sc in each sc around: 12 sc.

Rnd 3: (2 Sc in next sc, sc in next sc) around: 18 sc.

Rnd 4: (2 Sc in next sc, sc in next 2 sc) around: 24 sc.

Rnd 5: Sc in each sc around.

Rnd 6: (2 Sc in next sc, sc in next 3 sc) around: 30 sc.

Rnds 7-9: Sc in each sc around.

Rnd 10: (Sc2tog, sc in next 3 sc) around: 24 sc.

Rnd 11: (Sc2tog, sc in next 4 sc) around: 20 sc.

Rnd 12: Sc in each sc around.

Rnd 13: (Sc2tog, sc in next 3 sc) around: 16 sc.

Rnd 14: (Sc2tog, sc in next 2 sc) around: 12 sc.

Rnd 15: (Sc2tog, sc in next 4 sc) twice: 10 sc.

Stuff Head with polyester fiberfill.

Rnds 16-19: Sc in each sc around.

Rnd 20: (2 Sc in next sc, sc in next sc) around: 15 sc.

Rnd 21: (2 Sc in next sc, sc in next 2 sc) around: 20 sc.

Rnd 22: (2 Sc in next sc, sc in next 3 sc) around: 25 sc.

Rnds 23 and 24: (2 Sc in next sc, sc in next 4 sc) around: 36 sc.

Rnds 25-30: Sc in each sc around.

Rnd 31: (Sc2tog, sc in next 4 sc) around: 30 sc.

Rnd 32: (Sc2tog, sc in next 3 sc) around: 24 sc.

Rnd 33: (Sc2tog, sc in next 2 sc) around: 18 sc.

Rnd 34: (Sc2tog, sc in next sc) around: 12 sc.

Stuff Body with polyester fiberfill.

Rnd 35: Sc2tog around; slip st in next sc, finish off leaving a 6" (15 cm) length for sewing.

Thread yarn needle with end and weave yarn through Front Loop Only of remaining sc to close ***(Fig. 4, page 48)***; secure end.

ARM (Make 2)

Rnd 1 (Right side)**:** With Brown, make an adjustable ring, 5 sc in ring; do **not** join, place marker to indicated the beginning of the round.

Note: Mark Rnd 1 as **right** side.

Rnd 2: 2 Sc in each sc around: 10 sc.

Rnd 3: (2 Sc in next sc, sc in next 4 sc) twice: 12 sc.

Rnd 4: Sc in each sc around changing to Gold in last sc ***(Fig. 6b, page 49)***; cut Brown.

Rnd 5: Sc in each sc around.

Rnd 6: (Sc2tog, sc in next 4 sc) twice: 10 sc.

Rnds 7-10: Sc in each sc around.

Rnd 11: (Sc2tog, sc in next 3 sc) twice: 8 sc.

Stuff Arm with polyester fiberfill, to within ½" (12 mm) of opening.

Joining Row: Ch 1; flatten top of Arm having ch at fold. Working through **both** loops of **both** sides ***(Fig. 4, page 48)***, sc in each sc across; finish off leaving an 8" (20.5 cm) length for sewing.

FOOT & LEG (Make 2)

Rnd 1 (Right side)**:** With Brown, make an adjustable ring, 5 sc in ring; do **not** join, place marker to indicated the beginning of the round.

Note: Mark Rnd 1 as **right** side.

Rnd 2: 2 Sc in each sc around: 10 sc.

Rnd 3: (2 Sc in next sc, sc in next sc) around: 15 sc.

Rnd 4: Sc in each sc around changing to Gold in last sc; cut Brown.

Rnds 5 and 6: Sc in each sc around.

Rnd 7: (Sc2tog, sc in next 3 sc) around: 12 sc.

Rnds 8-10: Sc in each sc around.

Rnd 11: (Sc2tog, sc in next 4 sc) twice: 10 sc.

Rnd 12: Sc in each sc around.

Stuff Leg with polyester fiberfill.

Joining Row: Ch 1; flatten top of Leg having ch at fold. Working through **both** loops of **both** sides, sc in each sc across; finish off leaving an 8" (20.5 cm) length for sewing.

MUZZLE

Rnd 1 (Right side)**:** With Gold, make an adjustable ring, 6 sc in ring; do **not** join, place marker to indicated the beginning of the round.

Note: Mark Rnd 1 as **right** side.

Rnd 2: (2 Sc in next sc, sc in next sc) 3 times: 9 sc.

Rnd 3: (2 Sc in next sc, sc in next 2 sc) 3 times: 12 sc.

Rnd 4: Sc in each sc around.

Rnd 5: Sc in next 6 sc, hdc in next sc, 2 hdc in next sc, hdc in next sc, sc in next 3 sc: 13 sts.

Rnd 6: Slip st in next 7 sts; finish off leaving a 10" (25.5 cm) length for sewing.

EAR (Make 2)

Rnd 1 (Right side)**:** With Gold, make an adjustable ring, 5 sc in ring; do **not** join, place marker to indicated the beginning of the round.

Note: Mark Rnd 1 as **right** side.

Rnd 2: 2 Sc in next sc, sc in next sc, 2 sc in next sc, sc in next 2 sc: 7 sc.

Rnd 3: Sc in next sc, (2 sc in next sc, sc in next sc) 3 times: 10 sc.

Rnd 4: Sc in each sc around.

Rnd 5: (Sc2tog twice, sc in next sc) twice; slip st in next sc, finish off leaving an 8" (20.5 cm) length for sewing.

HORN (Make 2)

Rnd 1 (Right side)**:** With Gold, make an adjustable ring, 4 sc in ring; do **not** join, place marker to indicated the beginning of the round.

Note: Mark Rnd 1 as **right** side.

Rnds 2-4: Sc in each sc around; at end of Rnd 4, slip st in next sc changing to Brown ***(Fig. 6a, page 49)***, cut Gold.

Rnd 5: Ch 2, ★ YO, insert hook in **same** st as slip st, YO and pull up a loop, YO and draw through 2 loops on hook; repeat from ★ 3 times **more**, YO and draw through all 5 loops on hook, ch 1, skip next sc, slip st in next sc, finish off.

TAIL

With Gold, ch 6; slip st in back ridge of second ch from hook and each ch across ***(Fig. 3, page 48)***; finish off.

Add three, 3" (7.5 cm) lengths of Brown as fringe to end of Tail ***(Figs. 7a & b, page 49)***; trim ends and separate plies.

FINISHING

Using Photo as a guide for placement:

- Sew Arms to Body across Rnds 19-23.
- Sew Legs to bottom of Body across Rnds 30-35, so Giraffe is in a seated position.
- With Black, add straight stitch nostrils to Muzzle ***(Fig. 9, page 50)***.
- Stuff Muzzle with polyester fiberfill and sew Muzzle to Head across Rnds 9-12.
- Flatten Ear having end at fold; sew fold on each side of last rnd together and sew to each side of Head, across Rnds 5 and 6.
- Sew Horns to top of Head between Ears.
- Sew Tail between Rnds 31 and 32 at center back of Body.
- With Black, add satin stitch eyes across Rnds 7 and 8 ***(Fig. 8a, page 50)***.
- With Brown, add satin stitch patches to Giraffe ***(Fig. 8b, page 50)***.

Lion

EASY

Finished Size: 6" (15 cm) tall (seated)

SHOPPING LIST

Yarn (Medium Weight) 

[7 ounces, 364 yards

(198 grams, 333 meters) per skein]:

- ☐ Gold - 100 yards (91.5 meters)
- ☐ Rust - 10 yards (9 meters)
- ☐ White - 8 yards (7.3 meters)
- ☐ Brown - 1 yard (.9 meter)
- ☐ Brown - 1 yard (.9 meter)

Crochet Hook

- ☐ Size G (4 mm)

  or size needed for gauge

Additional Supplies

- ☐ Polyester fiberfill
- ☐ Yarn needle

GAUGE INFORMATION

8 sc and 8 rows = 2" (5 cm)

Gauge Swatch: 2" (5 cm) square

Ch 9.

Row 1: Sc in second ch from hook and in each ch across: 8 sc.

Rows 2-8: Ch 1, turn; sc in each sc across.

Finish off.

STITCH GUIDE

SINGLE CROCHET 2 TOGETHER

(abbreviated sc2tog)

Pull up a loop in each of next 2 sts, YO and draw through all 3 loops on hook **(counts as one sc)** ***(Fig. A)***.

Fig. A

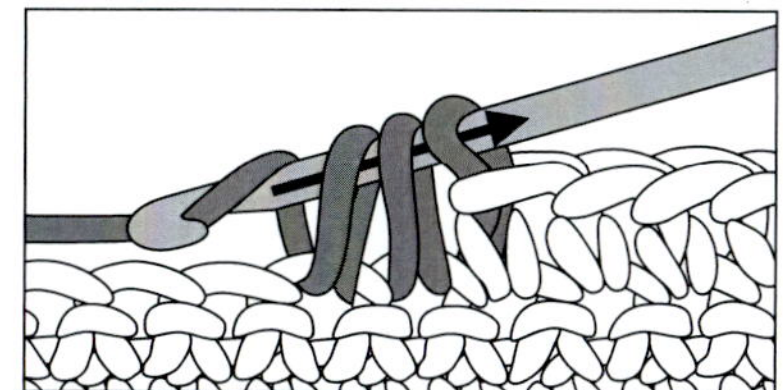

HEAD & BODY

Rnd 1 (Right side)**:** With Gold, make an adjustable ring *(Figs. 2a-d, pages 48)*, 6 sc in ring; do **not** join, place marker to indicated the beginning of the round *(see Markers, page 48)*.

Note: Loop a short piece of yarn around any stitch to mark Rnd 1 as **right** side.

Rnd 2: 2 Sc in each sc around: 12 sc.

Rnd 3: (2 Sc in next sc, sc in next sc) around: 18 sc.

Rnd 4: (2 Sc in next sc, sc in next 2 sc) around: 24 sc.

Rnd 5: (2 Sc in next sc, sc in next 3 sc) around: 30 sc.

Rnds 6-10: Sc in each sc around.

Rnd 11: (Sc2tog, sc in next 3 sc) around: 24 sc.

Rnd 12: (Sc2tog, sc in next 2 sc) around: 18 sc.

Rnd 13: (Sc2tog, sc in next sc) around: 12 sc.

Stuff Head with polyester fiberfill.

Rnd 14: (2 Sc in next sc, sc in next sc) around: 18 sc.

Rnd 15: (2 Sc in next sc, sc in next 2 sc) around: 24 sc.

Rnd 16: (2 Sc in next sc, sc in next 3 sc) around: 30 sc.

Rnd 17: (2 Sc in next sc, sc in next 4 sc) around: 36 sc.

Rnds 18-25: Sc in each sc around.

Rnd 26: (Sc2tog, sc in next 4 sc) around: 30 sc.

Rnd 27: (Sc2tog, sc in next 3 sc) around: 24 sc.

Rnd 28: (Sc2tog, sc in next 2 sc) around: 18 sc.

Rnd 29: (Sc2tog, sc in next sc) around: 12 sc.

Stuff Body with polyester fiberfill.

Rnd 29: Sc2tog around; slip st in next sc, finish off leaving a 6" (15 cm) length for sewing.

Thread yarn needle with end and weave yarn through Front Loop Only of remaining sc to close *(Fig. 4, page 48)*; secure end.

FOOT & LEG (Make 2)

Rnd 1 (Right side)**:** With Gold, make an adjustable ring, 6 sc in ring; do **not** join, place marker to indicated the beginning of the round.

Note: Mark Rnd 1 as **right** side.

Rnd 2: 2 Sc in each sc around: 12 sc.

Rnd 3: (2 Sc in next sc, sc in next sc) around: 18 sc.

Rnd 4: (2 Sc in next sc, sc in next 2 sc) around: 24 sc.

Rnd 5: Sc in each sc around.

Rnd 6: Sc in next 12 sc, (sc2tog, sc in next 2 sc) 3 times: 21 sc.

Rnd 7: Sc in next 13 sc, sc2tog 4 times: 17 sc.

Rnd 8: Sc in each sc around.

Rnd 9: Sc in next 11 sc, sc2tog 3 times: 14 sc.

Rnd 10: Sc2tog, (sc in next 2 sc, sc2tog) 3 times: 10 sc.

Stuff Foot with polyester fiberfill.

Rnds 11 and 12: Sc in each sc around.

Rnd 13: Sc in next 8 sc; ch 1, flatten top of Leg having ch at fold. Working through **both** loops of **both** pieces ***(Fig. 4, page 48)***, sc in each sc across; finish off leaving an 8" (20.5 cm) length for sewing.

ARM (Make 2)

Rnd 1 (Right side)**:** With Gold, make an adjustable ring, 6 sc in ring; do **not** join, place marker to indicated the beginning of the round.

Note: Mark Rnd 1 as **right** side.

Rnd 2: 2 Sc in each sc around: 12 sc.

Rnd 3: (2 Sc in next sc, sc in next sc) around: 18 sc.

Rnds 4 and 5: Sc in each sc around.

Rnd 6 (Decrease rnd)**:** (Sc2tog, sc in next sc) around: 12 sc.

Rnds 7-9: Repeat Rnds 4-6: 8 sc.

Stuff Arm with polyester fiberfill.

Rnds 10 and 11: Sc in each sc around.

Joining Row: Ch 1; flatten top of Arm having ch at fold. Working through **both** loops of **both** pieces, sc in each sc across; finish off leaving an 8" (20.5 cm) length for sewing.

EAR (Make 2)

Rnd 1 (Right side)**:** With Gold, make an adjustable ring, 5 sc in ring; do **not** join, place marker to indicated the beginning of the round.

Note: Mark Rnd 1 as **right** side.

Rnd 2: 2 Sc in each sc around: 10 sc.

Rnd 3: (2 Sc in next sc, sc in next sc) around: 15 sc.

Rnd 4: Sc in each sc around; slip st in next sc, finish off leaving a 6" (15 cm) length for sewing.

MUZZLE

Rnd 1 (Right side)**:** With White, make an adjustable ring, 6 sc in ring; do **not** join, place marker to indicated the beginning of the round.

Note: Mark Rnd 1 as **right** side.

Rnd 2: 2 Sc in each sc around: 12 sc.

Rnd 3: 2 Sc in next sc, sc in next sc, 2 sc in next sc, hdc in next sc, (2 hdc in next sc, hdc in next sc) twice, (2 sc in next sc, sc in next sc) twice: 18 sts.

Rnd 4: Sc in each sc around; slip st in next sc, finish off leaving a 12" (30.5 cm) length for sewing.

Using satin stitch ***(Figs. 8a & b, page 50)***, add Brown Nose; then using straight stitch ***(Fig. 9, page 50)***, add features.

TAIL

With Brown, ch 4; working in back ridge of chs ***(Fig. 3, page 48)***, sc in second ch from hook, hdc in last 2 chs; finish off leaving a 6" (15 cm) length for sewing.

Cut two, 2" (5 cm) strands of Rust.

Holding strands together, fold in half. Draw the folded end up through unworked ch at end of Tail, pull loose ends through folded end; draw the knot up tightly.

Trim to ½" (12 mm).

FINISHING

Using Photo as a guide for placement:

- Sew Muzzle to Head.
- Sew one Arm to each side of Body across Rnds 15-17.
- Sew one Ear to each side of Head.
- Sew Legs to Body so Lion is in a seated position; sew Tail to back of Body.
- Using satin stitch, add Black eyes.
- Using turkey loop stitch ***(Fig. 10, page 50)***, add Rust Mane around Face. Cut loops and fluff Mane.

Tiger

EASY

Finished Size: 6" (15 cm) tall (seated)

SHOPPING LIST

Yarn (Medium Weight) 

[7 ounces, 364 yards
(198 grams, 333 meters) per skein**]**:

- ☐ Orange - 65 yards (59.5 meters)
- ☐ Black - 22 yards (20 meters)
- ☐ Off White - 10 yards (9 meters)

Crochet Hook

- ☐ Size G (4 mm)
  or size needed for gauge

Additional Supplies

- ☐ Polyester fiberfill
- ☐ Yarn needle

GAUGE INFORMATION

8 sc and 8 rows = 2" (5 cm)

Gauge Swatch: 2" (5 cm) square

Ch 9.

Row 1: Sc in second ch from hook and in each ch across: 8 sc.

Rows 2-8: Ch 1, turn; sc in each sc across.

Finish off.

STITCH GUIDE

SINGLE CROCHET 2 TOGETHER
(abbreviated sc2tog)

Pull up a loop in each of next 2 sts, YO and draw through all 3 loops on hook **(counts as one sc)** ***(Fig. A)***.

Fig. A

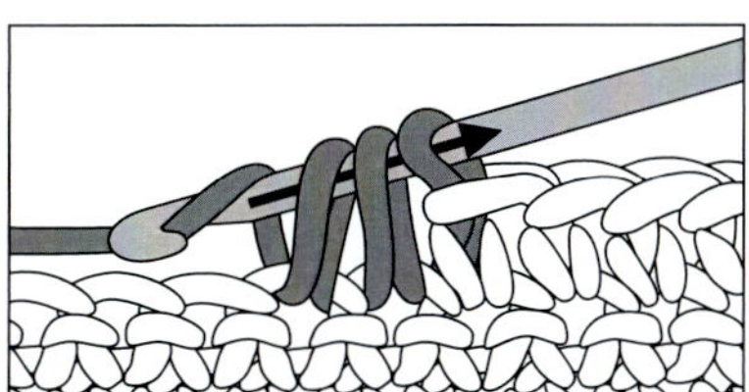

HEAD & BODY

Rnd 1 (Right side)**:** With Orange, make an adjustable ring ***(Figs. 2a-d, pages 48)***, 6 sc in ring; do **not** join, place marker to indicated the beginning of the round ***(see Markers, page 48)***.

Note: Loop a short piece of yarn around any stitch to mark Rnd 1 as **right** side.

Rnd 2: 2 Sc in each sc around: 12 sc.

Rnd 3: (2 Sc in next sc, sc in next sc) around: 18 sc.

Rnd 4: (2 Sc in next sc, sc in next 2 sc) around, changing to Black in last sc made ***(Fig. 6b, page 49)***, drop Orange to **wrong** side of work: 24 sc.

Rnd 5: (2 Sc in next sc, sc in next 3 sc) around, changing to Orange in last sc made, drop Black to **wrong** side of work: 30 sc.

Rnds 6 and 7: Sc in each sc around, changing to Black in last sc made on Rnd 7, drop Orange to **wrong** side of work.

Rnd 8: Sc in each sc around, changing to Orange in last sc made, drop Black to **wrong** side of work.

Rnds 9 and 10: Sc in each sc around, changing to Black in last sc made on Rnd 10, drop Orange to **wrong** side of work.

Rnd 11: (Sc2tog, sc in next 3 sc) around, changing to Orange in last sc made, drop Black to **wrong** side of work: 24 sc.

Rnd 12: (Sc2tog, sc in next 2 sc) around: 18 sc.

Rnd 13: (Sc2tog, sc in next sc) around: 12 sc.

Stuff Head with polyester fiberfill.

Rnd 14: (2 Sc in next sc, sc in next sc) around: 18 sc.

Rnd 15: (2 Sc in next sc, sc in next 2 sc) around, changing to Black in last sc made, drop Orange to **wrong** side of work: 24 sc.

Rnd 16: (2 Sc in next sc, sc in next 3 sc) around, changing to Orange in last sc made, drop Black to **wrong** side of work: 30 sc.

Rnd 17: (2 Sc in next sc, sc in next 4 sc) around: 36 sc.

Rnd 18: Sc in each sc around, changing to Black in last sc made, drop Orange to **wrong** side of work.

Rnd 19: Sc in each sc around, changing to Orange in last sc made, drop Black to **wrong** side of work.

Rnds 20 and 21: Sc in each sc around, changing to Black in last sc made on Rnd 21, drop Orange to **wrong** side of work.

Rnd 22: Sc in each sc around, changing to Orange in last sc made, drop Black to **wrong** side of work.

Rnd 23: Sc in each sc around.

Rnd 24: (Sc2tog, sc in next 4 sc) around, changing to Black in last sc made, drop Orange to **wrong** side of work: 30 sc.

Rnd 25: (Sc2tog, sc in next 3 sc) around, changing to Orange in last sc made, cut Black: 24 sc.

Rnd 26: (Sc2tog, sc in next 2 sc) around: 18 sc.

Rnd 27: (Sc2tog, sc in next sc) around: 12 sc.

Stuff Body with polyester fiberfill.

Rnd 28: Sc2tog around; slip st in next sc, finish off leaving a 6" (15 cm) length for sewing.

Thread yarn needle with end and weave yarn through Front Loops Only of remaining sc ***(Fig. 4, page 48)***; secure end.

FOOT & LEG (Make 2)

Rnd 1 (Right side)**:** With Orange, make an adjustable ring, 5 sc in ring; do **not** join, place marker to indicated the beginning of the round.

Note: Mark Rnd 1 as **right** side.

Rnd 2: 2 Sc in each sc around: 10 sc.

Rnd 3: (Sc in next sc, 2 sc in next sc) around: 15 sc.

Rnds 4 and 5: Sc in each sc around; at end of Rnd 5, change to Black in last sc made, drop Orange to **wrong** side of work.

Rnd 6: Sc in each sc around, changing to Orange in last sc made, drop Black to **wrong** side of work.

Rnds 7 and 8: Sc in each sc around; at end of Rnd 8, change to Black in last sc made, drop Orange to **wrong** side of work.

Rnd 9: Sc in each sc around changing to Orange in last sc made, cut Black.

Rnd 10: Sc in each sc around.

Rnd 11: (Sc2tog, sc in next sc) around: 10 sc.

Stuff Leg lightly with polyester fiberfill.

Joining Row: Ch 1; flatten top of Leg having ch fold. Working through **both** loops of **both** sides *(Fig. 4, page 48)*, sc in each sc across; finish off leaving a 8" (20.5 cm) end for sewing.

ARM (Make 2)

Rnd 1 (Right side): With Orange, make an adjustable ring, 5 sc in ring; do **not** join, place marker to indicated the beginning of the round.

Note: Mark Rnd 1 as **right** side.

Rnd 2: 2 Sc in each sc around: 10 sc.

Rnd 3: (Sc in next 4 sc, 2 sc in next sc) twice: 12 sc.

Rnd 4: Sc in each sc around, changing to Black in last sc, drop Orange to **wrong** side of work.

Rnd 5: Sc in each sc around, changing to Orange in last sc, drop Black to wrong **side** of work.

Rnds 6 and 7: Sc in each sc around; at end of Rnd 7, change to Black in last sc made, drop Orange to **wrong** side of work.

Rnd 8: Sc in each sc around, changing to Orange in last sc, cut Black.

Rnd 9: Sc in each sc around.

Rnd 10: (Sc2tog, sc in next sc) around: 8 sc.

Stuff Arm lightly with polyester fiberfill.

Joining Row: Ch 1; flatten top of Arm having ch fold. Working through **both** loops of **both** sides, sc in each sc across; finish off leaving a 8" (20.5 cm) end for sewing.

EAR (Make 2)

Row 1 (Right side)**:** With Orange and leaving a 6" (15 cm) length for gathering, ch 2, 3 sc in second ch from hook; do **not** join.

Note: Mark Row 1 as **right** side.

Row 2: Ch 1, turn; 2 sc in each sc across: 6 sc.

Row 3: Ch 1, turn; sc in first 2 sc, 2 sc in each of next 2 sc, sc in last 2 sc; slip st in first sc of Row 3 to form base of Ear, finish off leaving an 8" (20.5 cm) end for sewing.

Gather end of rows (base of Ear) with beginning yarn; secure end.

MUZZLE

Rnd 1 (Right side)**:** With Off White, ch 4, 2 sc in second ch from hook, sc in next ch, 3 sc in last ch; working in free loops of beginning ch ***(Fig. 3, page 48)***, sc in next 2 chs; do **not** join, place marker to indicate the beginning of the round: 8 sc.

Note: Mark Rnd 1 as **right** side.

Rnd 2: 2 Sc in each of next 2 sc, 2 hdc in next sc, 2 sc in each of next 3 sc, 2 hdc in next sc, 2 sc in next sc: 16 sts.

Rnd 3: Sc in each st around, changing to Orange in last sc, cut Off White.

Rnd 4: Working in Front Loops Only, sc in next sc, 2 sc in each of next 2 sc, (sc, hdc) in next sc, 2 dc in each of next 4 sc, (hdc, sc) in next sc, 2 sc in each of next 2 sc, sc in next 5 sts: 26 sts.

Rnd 5: Working in both loops, sc in next 7 sts, 2 sc in next dc, sc in next 2 dc, 2 sc in each of next 2 dc, sc in next 2 dc, 2 sc in next dc, sc in next 7 sts, slip st in next 4 sc; finish off leaving a 12" (30.5 cm) length for sewing.

CHEST

With Off White, ch 6.

Rnd 1 (Right side)**:** 3 Hdc in second ch from hook, hdc in next 3 chs, 5 hdc in last ch; working in free loops of beginning ch, hdc in next 3 chs, 2 hdc in next ch; join with slip st to first hdc: 16 hdc.

Note: Mark Rnd 1 as **right** side.

Rnd 2: Ch 1, 2 hdc in same st as joining and in next hdc, dc in next 5 hdc, 2 hdc in each of next 3 hdc, dc in next 5 hdc, 2 hdc in last hdc; join with slip st to first hdc: 22 sts.

Rnd 3: Ch 1, sc in same st as joining and in next 3 hdc, 2 sc in next dc, sc in next 5 sts, 2 sc in next hdc, sc in next 4 hdc, 2 sc in next dc, sc in next 5 sts, 2 sc in last hdc; join with slip st to first sc, finish off leaving a 12" (30.5 cm) length for sewing.

TAIL

Rnd 1 (Right side)**:** With Orange, make an adjustable ring, 4 sc in ring; do **not** join, place marker to indicated the beginning of the round.

Note: Mark Rnd 1 as **right** side.

Rnd 2: (2 Sc in next sc, sc in next sc) twice: 6 sc.

Rnds 3-5: Sc in each sc around; at end of Rnd 5, change to Black in last sc, drop Orange to **wrong** side of work.

Rnd 6: Sc in each sc around, changing to Orange in last sc, drop Black to **wrong** side of work.

Rnds 7-9: Sc in each sc around; at end of Rnd 9, change to Black in last sc, drop Orange to **wrong** side of work.

Rnd 10: Sc in each sc around, changing to Orange in last sc, cut Black.

Rnds 11-13: Sc in each sc around; at end of Rnd 13, slip st in next sc and finish off leaving a 6" (15 cm) length for sewing.

FINISHING

Using Photo as a guide for placement:

- Sew Muzzle to Head.
- Sew Chest to Body.
- Sew one Arm to each side of Body.
- Sew one Ear to each side of Head.
- Sew Legs to Body; sew Tail to back of Body.
- Using satin stitch ***(Figs. 8a & b, page 50)***, add Black eyes and Nostrils.
- Using straight stitch ***(Fig. 9, page 50)***, add Black claws to Arms & Legs; add Black whiskers.

Elephant

▰▰▱▱ **EASY**

Finished Size: 6" (15 cm) tall (seated)

SHOPPING LIST

Yarn (Medium Weight) 

[7 ounces, 359 yards
(200 grams, 328 meters) per skein]:

- ☐ Gray - 160 yards (146.5 meters)
- ☐ Pink - 4 yards (3.7 meters)

Crochet Hook

- ☐ Size G (4 mm)
  or size needed for gauge

Additional Supplies

- ☐ 12mm Safety eyes - 2
- ☐ Polyester fiberfill
- ☐ Yarn needle

GAUGE INFORMATION

8 sc and 8 rows = 2" (5 cm)

Gauge Swatch: 2" (5 cm) square

Ch 9.

Row 1: Sc in second ch from hook and in each ch across: 8 sc.

Rows 2-8: Ch 1, turn; sc in each sc across.

Finish off.

STITCH GUIDE

SINGLE CROCHET 2 TOGETHER

(abbreviated sc2tog)

Pull up a loop in each of next 2 sts, YO and draw through all 3 loops on hook **(counts as one sc)** ***(Fig. A)***.

Fig. A

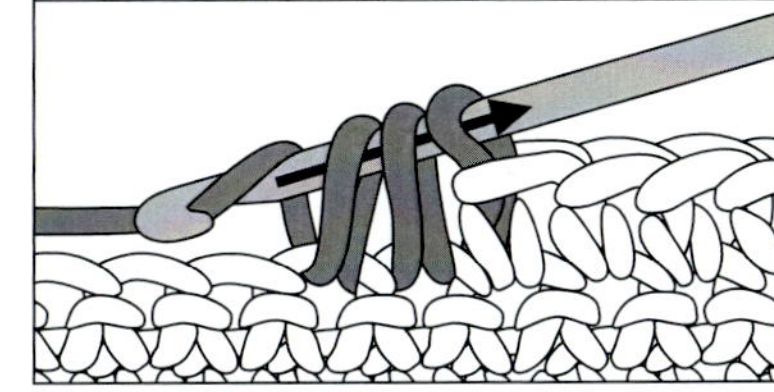

HALF DOUBLE CROCHET 2 TOGETHER

(abbreviated hdc2tog)

(uses next 2 sts)

★ YO, insert hook in **next** st, YO and pull up a loop; repeat from ★ once **more**, YO and draw through all 5 loops on hook **(counts as one hdc)** ***(Fig. B)***.

Fig. B

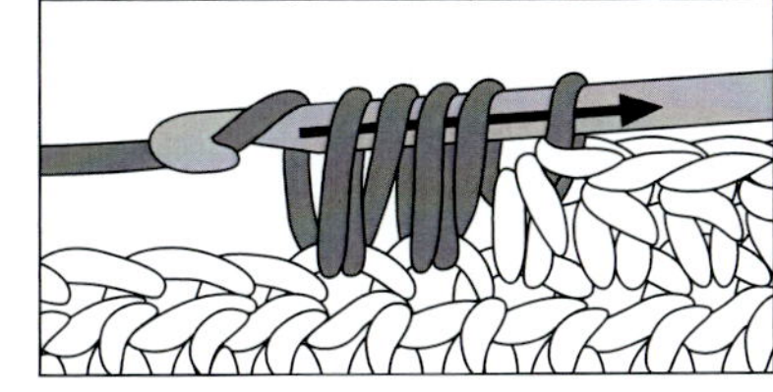

HALF DOUBLE CROCHET CLUSTER

(abbreviated hdc Cluster)

(uses one st)

YO, insert hook in st indicated, YO and pull up a loop (3 loops on hook), YO, insert hook in **same** st, YO and pull up a loop, YO and draw through all 5 loops on hook ***(Fig. C)***.

Fig. C

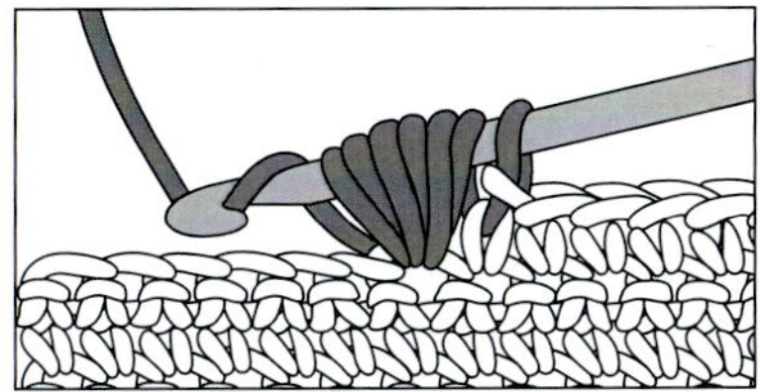

HEAD

Rnd 1 (Right side)**:** With Gray, make an adjustable ring ***(Figs. 2a-d, pages 48)***, work 6 sc in ring; do **not** join, place marker to indicate the beginning of the round ***(see Markers, page 48)***.

Note: Loop a short piece of yarn around any stitch to mark Rnd 1 as **right** side.

Rnd 2: 2 Sc in each sc around: 12 sc.

Rnd 3: (Sc in next sc, 2 sc in next sc) around: 18 sc.

Rnds 4 and 5: (Sc in next 2 sc, 2 sc in next sc) around: 32 sc.

Rnd 6: Sc in each sc around.

Rnd 7: (2 Sc in next sc, sc in next 3 sc) around: 40 sc.

Rnds 8 and 9: Sc in each sc around.

Rnd 10: (2 Sc in next sc, sc in next 7 sc) around: 45 sc.

Rnds 11-13: Sc in each sc around.

Add safety eyes between Rnds 9 and 10, having 5 to 6 sts between eyes.

Rnd 14: (Sc2tog, sc in next 3 sc) around: 36 sc.

Rnd 15: Sc in each sc around.

Rnd 16: (Sc2tog, sc in next 2 sc) around: 27 sc.

Rnd 17: Sc in each sc around.

Stuff Head with polyester fiberfill.

Rnds 18 and 19: (Sc2tog, sc in next sc) around: 12 sc.

Do **not** finish off.

BODY

Rnd 1 (Right side)**:** Sc in each sc around.

Rnd 2: (Sc in next sc, 2 sc in next sc) around: 18 sc.

Rnd 3: (2 Sc in next sc, sc in next 2 sc) around: 24 sc.

Rnd 4: Sc in each sc around.

Rnd 5: (2 Sc in next sc, sc in next 7 sc) around: 27 sc.

Rnds 6-8: Sc in each sc around.

Rnd 9: (2 Sc in next sc, sc in next 8 sc) around: 30 sc.

Rnds 10-13: Sc in each sc around.

Rnd 14: (Sc2tog, sc in next 3 sc) around: 24 sc.

Rnd 15: (Sc2tog, sc in next 2 sc) around: 18 sc.

Rnd 16: (Sc2tog, sc in next sc) around: 12 sc.

Stuff Body with polyester fiberfill.

Rnd 17: Sc2tog around; slip st in next sc and finish off, leaving an 8" (20.5 cm) length for sewing: 6 sts.

Thread yarn needle with yarn end and weave needle through Front Loops Only of remaining sts ***(Fig. 4, page 48)***; secure end.

LEG (Make 2)

Rnd 1 (Right side)**:** With Gray, make an adjustable ring, work 6 sc in ring; do **not** join, place marker to indicate the beginning of the round.

Note: Mark Rnd 1 as **right** side.

Rnd 2: 2 Sc in each sc around: 12 sc.

Rnd 3: (2 Sc in next sc, sc in next 2 sc) around: 16 sc.

Rnd 4: Sc in next 2 sc, 2 sc in next sc, (sc in next 3 sc, 2 sc in next sc) 3 times, sc in next sc; slip st in next sc: 20 sts.

Rnd 5: Ch 1, sc in Back Loop Only of same st as slip st and each sc around ***(Fig. 4, page 48)***; join with slip st to **both** loops of first sc.

Rnd 6: Ch 1, sc in same st as joining and in next 5 sc changing to Pink in last sc made ***(Fig. 6b, page 49)***, drop Gray to **wrong** side of work, work hdc Cluster in free loop of st one row **below** next sc (on Rnd 4) changing to Gray ***(Fig. 5a, page 49)***, skip sc **behind** hdc Cluster, ★ drop Pink to **wrong** side of work, sc in next sc changing to Pink, drop Gray to **wrong** side of work, work hdc Cluster in free loop of st one row **below** next sc (on Rnd 4) changing to Gray, skip sc **behind** hdc Cluster; repeat from ★ 2 times **more**, cut Pink, sc in last 7 sc; do **not** join, place marker to indicate the beginning of the round: 16 sc and 4 hdc Clusters.

Rnd 7 (Decrease rnd)**:** Sc2tog, sc in each st around: 19 sc.

Rnd 8: Sc in each sc around.

Rnds 9 and 10: Repeat Rnds 7 and 8: 18 sc.

Rnd 11: (Sc in next 4 sc, sc2tog) around: 15 sc.

Rnd 12: Sc in each sc around.

Rnd 13: (Sc in next 3 sc, sc2tog) around: 12 sc.

Rnds 14 and 15: Sc in each sc around.

Stuff Leg with polyester fiberfill to within ½" (12 mm) of opening.

Joining Row: Ch 1, flatten top of Leg having ch at fold; working through **both** loops of **both** sides ***(Fig. 4, page 48)***, sc in each sc across; finish off leaving an 8" (20.5 cm) length for sewing.

ARM (Make 2)

Rnd 1 (Right side)**:** With Gray, make an adjustable ring, work 6 sc in ring; do **not** join, place marker to indicate the beginning of the round.

Note: Mark Rnd 1 as **right** side.

Rnd 2: 2 Sc in each sc around: 12 sc.

Rnd 3: (2 Sc in next sc, sc in next sc) around; slip st in next sc: 18 sts.

Rnd 4: Ch 1, sc in Back Loop Only of same st as slip st and each sc around; join with slip st to **both** loops of first sc.

Rnd 5: Ch 1, sc in same st as joining and in next 4 sc changing to Pink in last sc made, drop Gray to **wrong** side of work, work hdc Cluster in free loop of st one row **below** next sc (on Rnd 3) changing to Gray, skip sc **behind** hdc Cluster, ★ drop Pink to **wrong** side of work, sc in next sc changing to Pink, drop Gray to **wrong** side of work, work hdc Cluster in free loop of st one row **below** next sc (on Rnd 3) changing to Gray, skip sc **behind** hdc Cluster; repeat from ★ once **more**, cut Pink, sc in last 8 sc; do **not** join, place marker to indicate the beginning of the round: 15 sc and 3 hdc Clusters.

Rnd 6 (Decrease rnd)**:** Sc2tog, sc in each st around: 17 sc.

Rnd 7: Sc in each sc around.

Rnds 8 and 9: Repeat Rnds 6 and 7: 16 sc.

Rnd 10: (Sc in next 2 sc, sc2tog) around: 12 sc.

Rnd 11-13: Sc in each sc around.

Stuff Arm with polyester fiberfill to within ½" (12 mm) of opening.

Joining Row: Sc in next 4 sc, ch 1; flatten top of Arm having ch at fold; working through **both** loops of **both** sides, sc in each sc across; finish off leaving an 8" (20.5 cm) length for sewing: 6 sc.

EAR (Make 2)

Row 1: With Gray, make an adjustable ring, work 5 sc in ring; do **not** join.

Row 2 (Right side)**:** Ch 1, turn; 2 sc in first sc and in each sc across: 10 sc.

Note: Mark Row 2 as **right** side.

Row 3: Ch 1, turn; sc in first sc, hdc in next sc, 2 dc in each of next 2 sc, hdc in next 2 sc, 2 dc in each of next 2 sc, hdc in next sc, sc in last sc: 14 sts.

Row 4: Ch 1, turn; sc in first sc, (dc, 2 tr) in next hdc ***(Figs. 15a & b, page 39)***, 3 tr in each of next 3 dc, hdc in next dc, hdc2tog, hdc in next dc, 3 tr in each of next 3 dc, (2 tr, dc) in next hdc, sc in last sc, work 3 sc evenly spaced across end of rows; join with slip st to first sc, finish off leaving an 8" (20.5 cm) length for sewing: 32 sts.

TRUNK

Rnd 1 (Right side)**:** With Gray, make an adjustable ring, work 5 sc in ring; join with slip st to first sc.

Note: Mark Rnd 1 as **right** side.

Rnd 2: Ch 1, sc in Back Loop Only of same st as joining and each sc around; join with slip st to **both** loops of first sc.

Rnd 3: Ch 1, sc in same st as joining and in each sc around; do **not** join, place marker to indicate the beginning of the round.

Rnd 4 (Increase rnd)**:** 2 Sc in next sc, sc in each sc around: 6 sc.

Rnd 5: Sc in each sc around.

Rnds 6-11: Repeat Rnds 4 and 5, 3 times: 9 sc.

Rnd 12 (Increase row)**:** (Sc in next 2 sc, 2 sc in next sc) around: 12 sc.

Rnd 13: Sc in each sc around.

Rnds 14 and 15: Repeat Rnds 12 and 13: 16 sc.

Slip st in next sc, finish off leaving a 10" (25.5 cm) length for sewing.

TAIL

Leaving a 2" (5 cm) length of Gray, ch 6 **tightly**; finish off leaving a 4" (10 cm) length for sewing.

FINISHING

Using Photo as a guide for placement and using long ends:

- Sew Arms to each side of Body, across Rnds 2-4.
- Sew Legs to bottom of Body across Rnds 14-17, so Elephant is in a seated position.
- Stuff Trunk with polyester fiberfill and sew to center of Head, across Rnds 11-16, centering between eyes.
- Sew Ears to each side of Head, across Rnds 7-13.
- Sew Tail to back of Body, between Rnds 13 and 14; separate plies of beginning ch and trim end as desired.

GENERAL INSTRUCTIONS

ABBREVIATIONS

ch(s)	chain(s)
cm	centimeters
dc	double crochet(s)
hdc	half double crochet(s)
hdc2tog	half double crochet 2 together
mm	millimeters
Rnd(s)	Round(s)
sc	single crochet(s)
sc2tog	single crochet 2 together
sp(s)	space(s)
st(s)	stitch(es)
tr	treble crochet(s)
YO	yarn over

SYMBOLS & TERMS

★ — work instructions following ★ as many **more** times as indicated in addition to the first time.

( ) or **[ ]** — work enclosed instructions **as many** times as specified by the number immediately following **or** work all enclosed instructions in the stitch or space indicated **or** contains explanatory remarks.

colon (:) — the number(s) given after a colon at the end of a row or round denote(s) the number of stitches you should have on that row or round.

CROCHET TERMINOLOGY		
UNITED STATES		INTERNATIONAL
slip stitch (slip st)	=	single crochet (sc)
single crochet (sc)	=	double crochet (dc)
half double crochet (hdc)	=	half treble crochet (htr)
double crochet (dc)	=	treble crochet (tr)
treble crochet (tr)	=	double treble crochet (dtr)
double treble crochet (dtr)	=	triple treble crochet (ttr)
triple treble crochet (tr tr)	=	quadruple treble crochet (qtr)
skip	=	miss

Yarn Weight Symbol & Names	LACE 0	SUPER FINE 1	FINE 2	LIGHT 3	MEDIUM 4	BULKY 5	SUPER BULKY 6	JUMBO 7
Type of Yarns in Category	Fingering, size 10 crochet thread	Sock, Fingering, Baby	Sport, Baby	DK, Light Worsted	Worsted, Afghan, Aran	Chunky, Craft, Rug	Super Bulky, Roving	Jumbo, Roving
Crochet Gauge* Ranges in Single Crochet to 4" (10 cm)	32-42 sts**	21-32 sts	16-20 sts	12-17 sts	11-14 sts	8-11 sts	6-9 sts	5 sts and fewer
Advised Hook Size Range	Steel*** 6 to 8, Regular hook B-1	B-1 to E-4	E-4 to 7	7 to I-9	I-9 to K-10½	K-10½ to M/N-13	M/N-13 to Q	Q and larger

*GUIDELINES ONLY: The chart above reflects the most commonly used gauges and hook sizes for specific yarn categories.

** Lace weight yarns are usually crocheted with larger hooks to create lacy openwork patterns. Accordingly, a gauge range is difficult to determine. Always follow the gauge stated in your pattern.

*** Steel crochet hooks are sized differently from regular hooks–the higher the number, the smaller the hook, which is the reverse of regular hook sizing.

BASIC	Projects using basic stitches. May include basic increases and decreases.
EASY	Projects may include simple stitch patterns, color work, and/or shaping.
INTERMEDIATE	Projects may include involved stitch patterns, color work, and/or shaping.
COMPLEX	Projects may include complex stitch patterns, color work, and/or shaping using a variety of techniques and stitches simultaneously.

CROCHET HOOKS																	
U.S.	B-1	C-2	D-3	E-4	F-5	G-6	7	H-8	I-9	J-10	K-10½	L-11	M/N-13	N/P-15	P/Q	Q	S
Metric - mm	2.25	2.75	3.25	3.5	3.75	4	4.5	5	5.5	6	6.5	8	9	10	15	16	19

GAUGE

Exact gauge is essential for proper size. Before beginning your project, make the sample swatch given in the instructions in the yarn and hook specified. After completing the swatch, measure it, counting your stitches and rows or rounds carefully. If your swatch is larger or smaller than specified, **make another, changing hook size to get the correct gauge**. Keep trying until you find the size hook that will give you the specified gauge.

MARKERS

Markers are used to help distinguish the beginning of each round being worked. Place a 2" (5 cm) scrap piece of yarn before the first stitch of each round, moving marker after each round is complete.

JOINING WITH A SC

When instructed to join with a sc, begin with a slip knot on hook. Insert hook in stitch or space indicated, YO and pull up a loop, YO and draw through both loops on hook.

Fig. 1

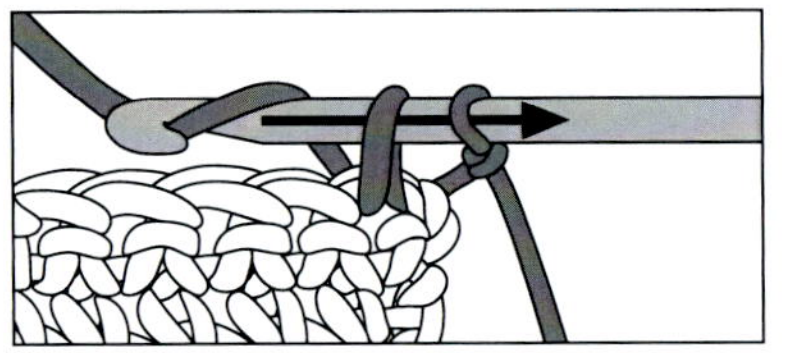

ADJUSTABLE RING

Wind the yarn around two fingers to form a ring ***(Fig. 2a)***.

Fig. 2a

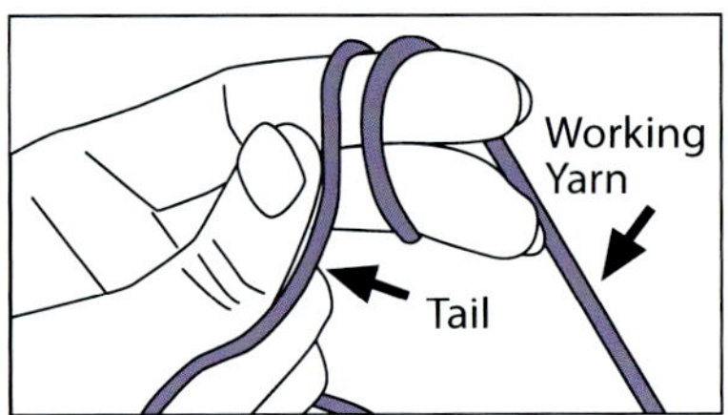

Slide the yarn off your fingers and grasp the strands at the top of the ring ***(Fig. 2b)***.

Fig. 2b

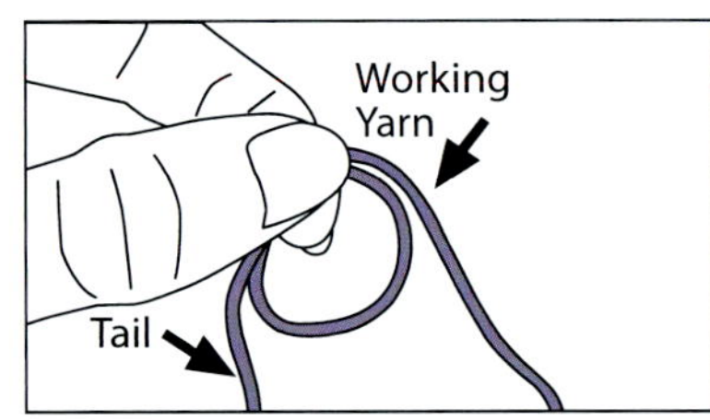

Insert the hook from **front** to **back** into the ring, pull up a loop, YO and draw through the loop on hook to lock the ring ***(Fig. 2c)***.

Fig. 2c

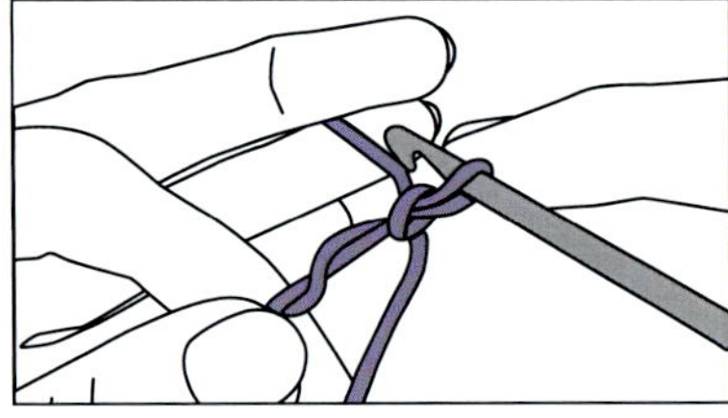

Working around both strands, work stitches in the ring as specified, then pull the yarn end to close ***(Fig. 2d)***.

Fig. 2d

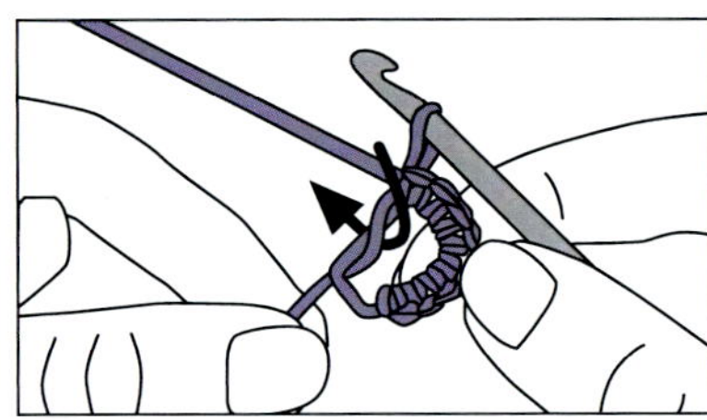

BACK RIDGE

Work only in loops indicated by arrows ***(Fig. 3)***.

Fig. 3

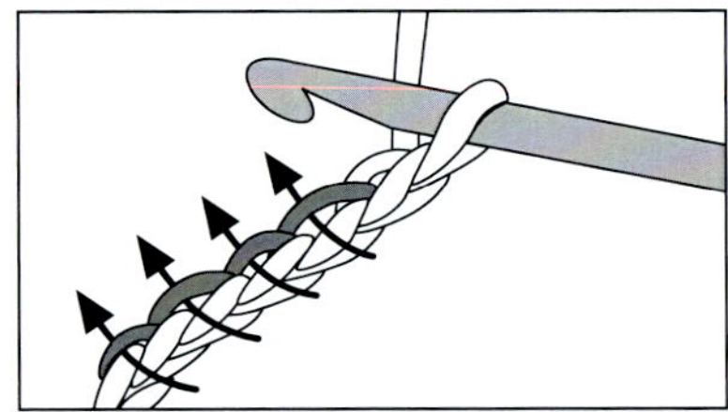

BACK OR FRONT LOOP ONLY

Work only in loops indicated by arrow ***(Fig. 4)***.

Fig. 4

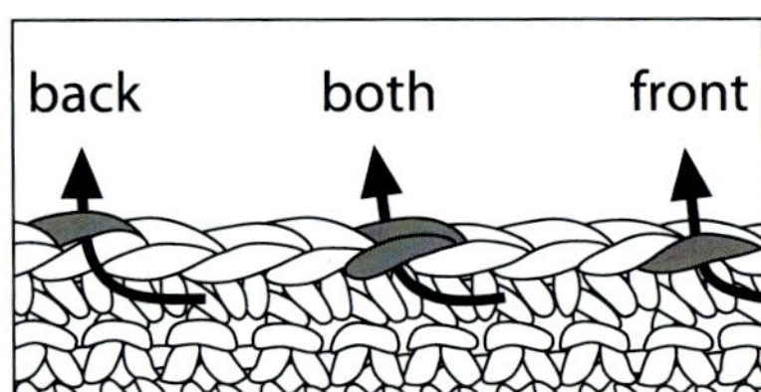

FREE LOOPS

After working in Back or Front Loops Only on a row or round, there will be a ridge of unused loop. These are called the free loops. Later, when instructed to work in the free loops of the same row or round, work in these loops ***(Fig. 5a)***.

Fig. 5a

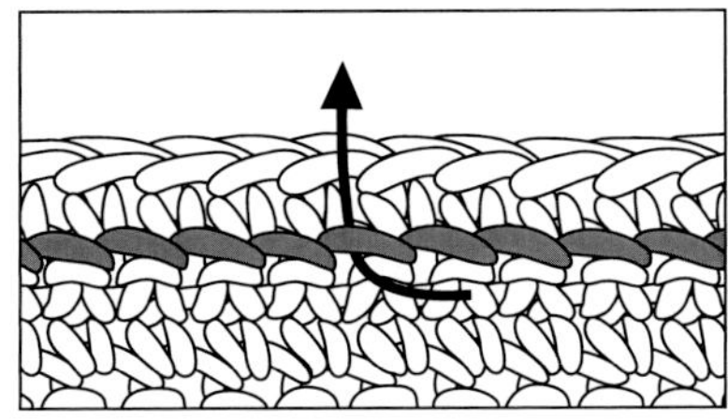

When instructed to work in free loops of a chain, work in loop indicated by arrow ***(Fig. 5b)***.

Fig. 5b

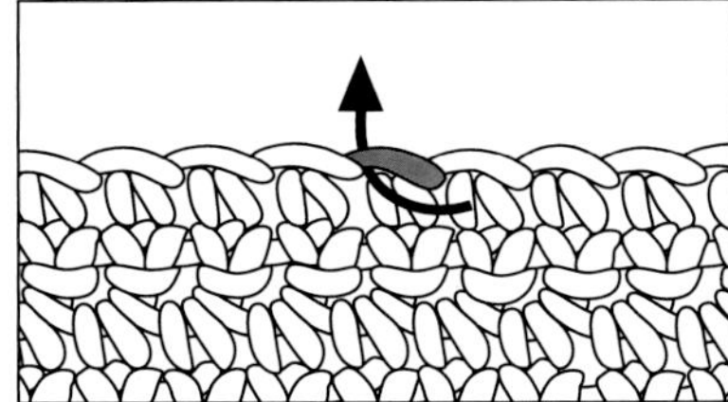

CHANGING COLORS

With A Slip St

Insert hook in st indicated, hook new color yarn and draw through all loops on hook ***(Fig. 6a)***.

Fig. 6a

In A Sc

Insert hook in st indicated, YO and pull up a loop, drop yarn; with new color yarn, YO and draw through both loops on hook ***(Fig. 6b)***.

Fig. 6b

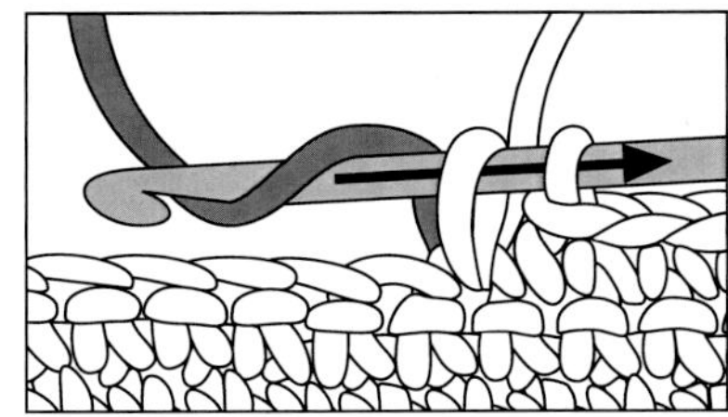

FRINGE

Cut a piece of cardboard 3" (7.5 cm) wide and ½" (12 mm) longer than you want your finished fringe to be. Wind the yarn **loosely** and **evenly** lengthwise around the cardboard until the card is filled, then cut across one end; repeat as needed.

Hold together as many strands as specified in individual instructions; fold in half.

With **wrong** side facing and using a crochet hook, draw the folded end up through a stitch, space, or row and pull the loose ends through the folded end ***(Fig. 7a)***; draw the knot up **tightly** ***(Fig. 7b)***.

Repeat spacing as specified in individual instructions.

Trim the ends.

Fig. 7a

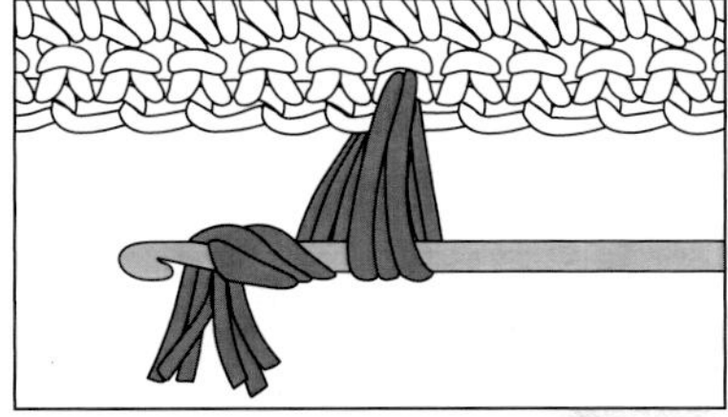

Fig. 7b

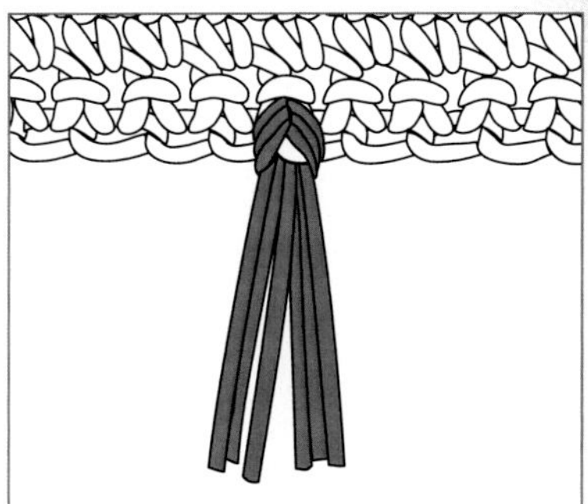

EMBROIDERY STITCHES

SATIN STITCH

Satin stitch is a series of straight stitches entering and exiting the same hole. Bring the needle up at 1 and go down at 2 ***(Fig. 8a)***.

Fig. 8a

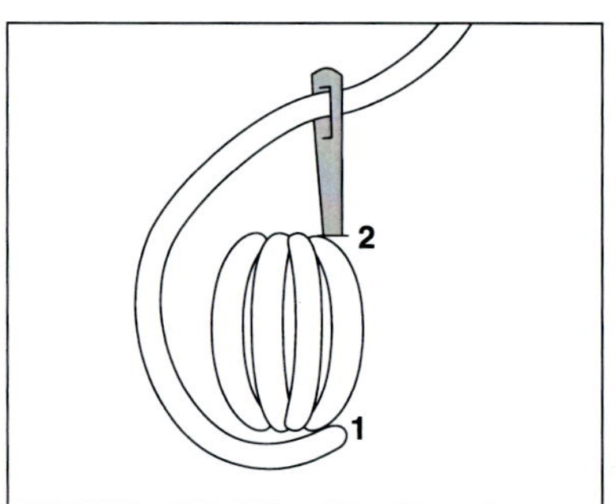

Satin stitch is also a series of straight stitches worked side-by-side, so they touch but do not overlap. Come up at odd numbers and go down at even numbers ***(Fig. 8b)***.

Fig. 8b

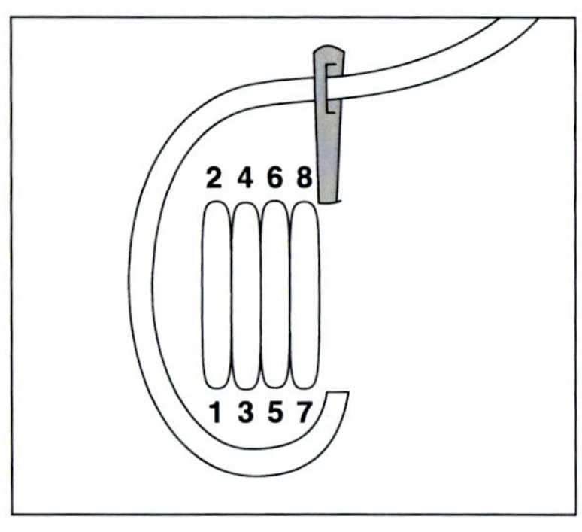

STRAIGHT STITCH

Straight stitch is just what the name implies, a single straight stitch. Come up at 1 and go down at 2 ***(Fig. 9)***.

Fig. 9

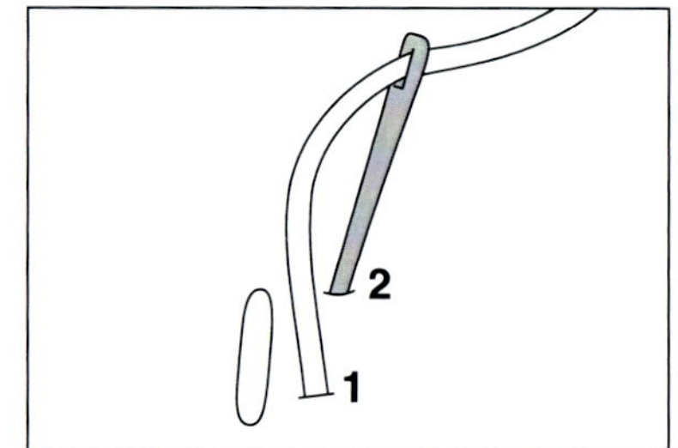

TURKEY LOOP STITCH

Bring the needle up at 1 and go down at 2 leaving a ¾ in. (1.9 cm) loop, come up at 3 and go down at 4 to secure loop ***(Fig. 10)***. Repeat for each loop.

Fig. 10

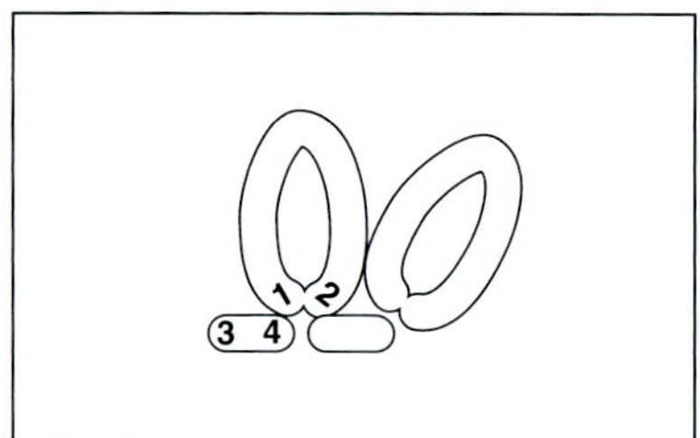

BASIC CROCHET STITCHES

SLIP STITCH

Insert hook in stitch indicated, YO and draw through stitch and through loop on hook ***(Fig. 11) (abbreviated slip st)***.

Fig. 11

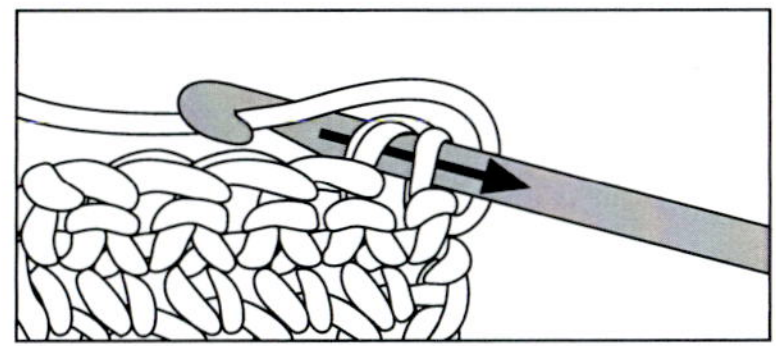

SINGLE CROCHET

Insert hook in stitch indicated, YO and pull up a loop, YO and draw through both loops on hook ***(Fig. 12) (abbreviated sc)***.

Fig. 12

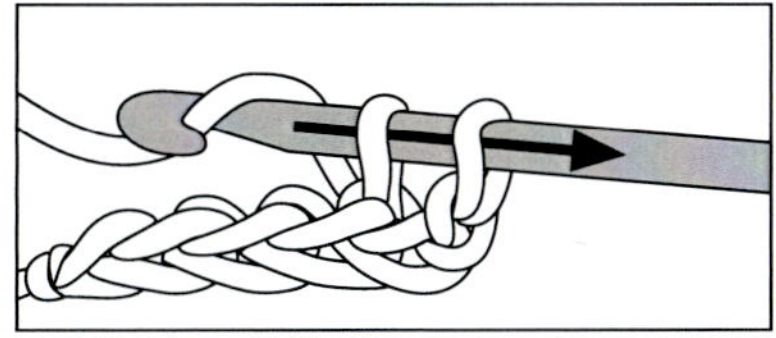

HALF DOUBLE CROCHET

YO, insert hook in stitch indicated, YO and pull up a loop, YO and draw through all 3 loops on hook ***(Fig. 13) (abbreviated hdc)***.

Fig. 13

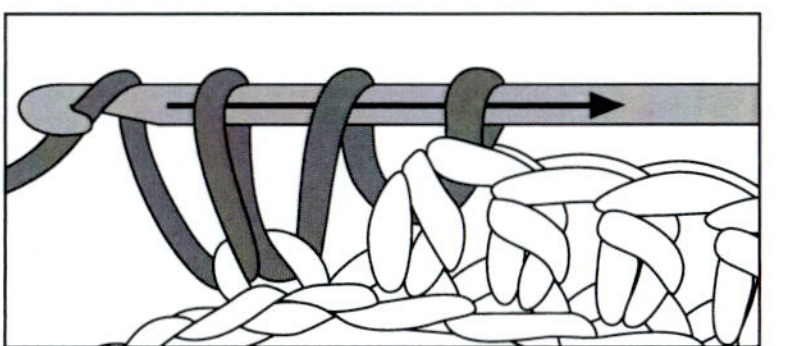

DOUBLE CROCHET

YO, insert hook in stitch indicated, YO and pull up a loop (3 loops on hook), YO and draw through 2 loops on hook ***(Fig. 14a)***, YO and draw through remaining 2 loops on hook ***(Fig. 14b) (abbreviated dc)***.

Fig. 14a

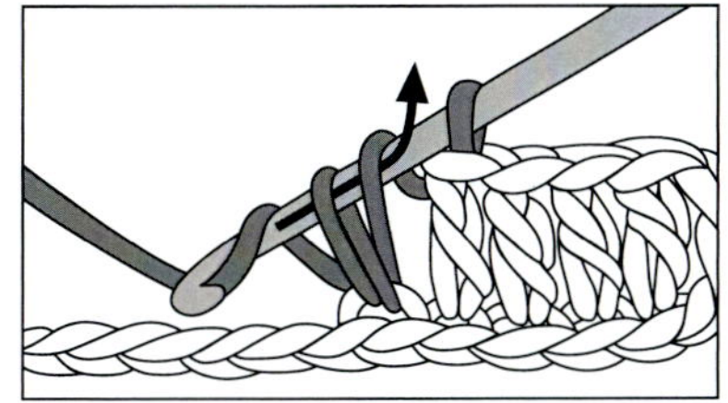

Fig. 14b

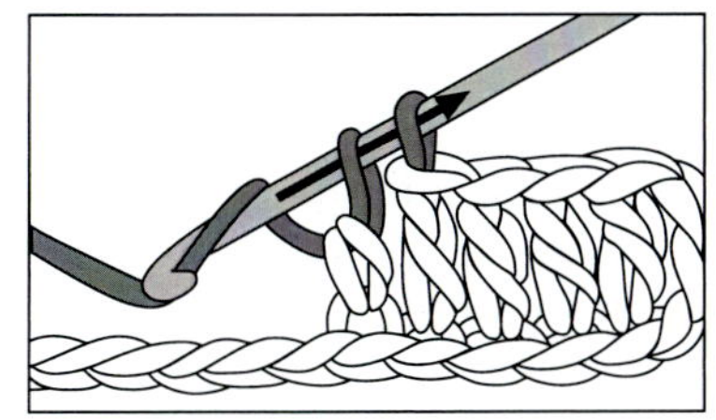

TREBLE CROCHET

YO twice, insert hook in stitch indicated, YO and pull up a loop (4 loops on hook) ***(Fig. 15a)***, (YO and draw through 2 loops on hook) 3 times ***(Fig. 15b) (abbreviated tr)***.

Fig. 15a

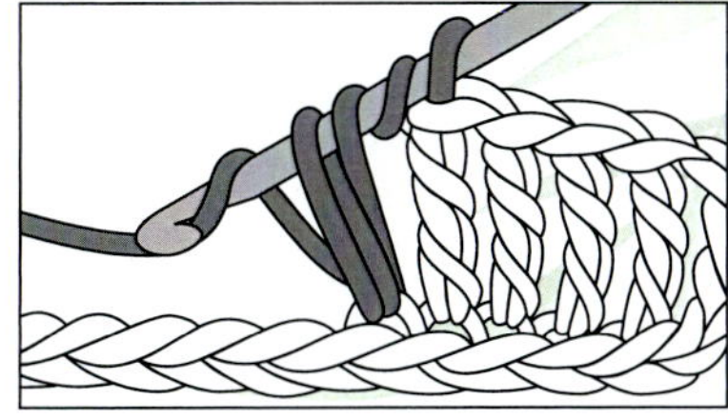

Fig. 15b

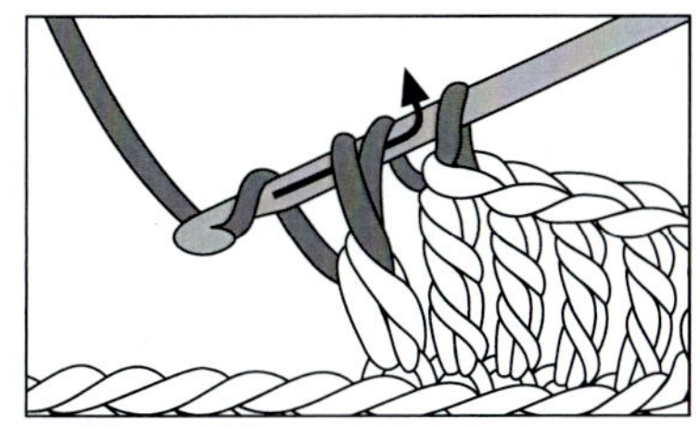

YARN INFORMATION

Each item in this book was made using Medium Weight Yarn except for the Monkey's banana which was made from Light Weight yarn. Any brand of the specified weight of yarn may be used. It is best to refer to the yardage/meters when determining how many balls or skeins to purchase. Remember, to arrive at the finished size, it is the GAUGE/TENSION that is important, not the brand of yarn.

For your convenience, listed below are the specific yarns used to create our photography models. Because yarn manufacturers make frequent changes to their product lines, you may sometimes find it necessary to use a substitute yarn or to search for the discontinued product at alternate suppliers (locallly or online).

MONKEY
Red Heart® Super Saver®
Brown - #0360 Cafe Latte
Tan - #0334 Buff
Patons® Astra™
Yellow - #02943 Maize Yellow
Off White - #02783 Aran
Black - #02765 Black

PANDA
Red Heart® Super Saver®
Black - #0312 Black
Soft White - #0316 Soft White
Green - #0624 Tea Leaf

BROWN BEAR
Red Heart® Soft®
Brown - #1882 Toast
Red Heart® Super Saver®
White - #0311 White
Black - #0312 Black

HIPPO
Red Heart® Super Saver®
Grey - #0340 Dusty Grey
Black - #0312 Black
Lt Grey - #0341 Light Grey

GIRAFFE
Red Heart® Super Saver®
Gold - #0321 Gold
Black - #0312 Black
Red Heart® Soft®
Brown - #1882 Toast

LION
Red Heart® Super Saver®
Gold - #0321 Gold
Rust - #0256 Carrot
White - #0311 White
Brown - #0360 Cafe Latte
Black - #0312 Black

TIGER
Red Heart® Super Saver®
Orange - #0256 Carrot
Black - #0312 Black
Off White - #0316 Soft White

ELEPHANT
Premier® Basix™
Gray - #1115-02 Light Gray
Pink - #1115-17 Light Mauve

Production Team: Project/Technical Editor - Linda A. Daley; Graphic Artist Christine DeLillo; and Photographer Rob Karman.

We have made every effort to ensure that these instructions are accurate and complete. We cannot, however, be responsible for human error, typographical mistakes, or variations in individual work.

Made in U.S.A.